Turn and Live

The Power of Repentance

Robert N. Wilkin

Grace Evangelical Society
Denton, Texas 76202

Turn and Live: The Power of Repentance

Copyright © 2019 by Grace Evangelical Society

Wilkin, Robert N., 1952—

ISBN 978-1-943399-34-5

All rights reserved. No part of this book may be reproduced in any form without the prior permission of the publisher, except as provided by USA copyright law.

All Scripture quotations, unless otherwise indicated, are taken from The Holy Bible New King James Version © 1982 by Thomas Nelson, Inc.

Requests for information should be sent to our mailing address:

Grace Evangelical Society
P.O. Box 1308
Denton, TX 76202
www.faithalone.org
ges@faithalone.org

Design: Shawn Lazar

Printed in the United States of America.

Dedicated to my lovely wife of 42 years, Sharon Dallas Wilkin.
Your impact on my life and ministry has been fantastic.
I am eternally grateful to you.

Contents

Preface 7
1. Why Study Repentance? 9
2. Repentance in Church History 13
3. Repentance in the Old Testament 21
4. The Meaning of Repentance in the New Testament 27
5. Repent for the Kingdom of Heaven Is at Hand
   (Matthew 3:2; 4:17) 31
6. Repent and Believe in the Gospel (Mark 1:14-15) 35
7. Unless You Repent You Will All Likewise Perish (Luke 13:3, 5) 39
8. If One Goes to Them from the Dead, They Will Repent
   (Luke 16:19-31) 43
9. Repentance and Forgiveness Should Be Preached (Luke 24:47) 47
10. Repent…and You Shall Receive the Gift of the Holy Spirit
    (Acts 2:38) 53
11. God Has Granted the Gentiles Repentance to Life (Acts 11:18) 59
12. Godly Sorrow Produces Repentance Leading to Salvation
    (2 Corinthians 7:10) 65
13. Turning to God from Idols (1 Thessalonians 1:9) 69
14. God Wishes None to Perish but for All to Repent (2 Peter 3:9) 73
15. Other Verses Thought to Link Salvation and Repentance 77
16. Repentance and the Gospel of John 85
17. Preaching Repentance and Salvation 89
18. Conclusion: Repentance Is a Vital Biblical Doctrine 93

Appendix 1: Why So Many Think Repentance
Is a Condition of Everlasting Life 99
Appendix 2: Why the Change-of-Mind View of Repentance
Is Inaccurate 105
Appendix 3: Righteous People Need No Repentance 113
Appendix 4: How We Can Have Assurance
That We Are in Fellowship with God 121
Appendix 5: Faith Alone in One Hundred Verses 131
Scripture Index 135
Subject Index 141
Study Guide 145

Preface

I wrote my doctoral dissertation, "Repentance and Salvation in the New Testament," at Dallas Theological Seminary from 1983 to 1985. I have since changed my view of repentance from the change-of-mind position to the turning-from-sins view.

There are very few books on repentance. Of the major books available in English, none of them give the New Testament the emphasis it deserves. (Zane Hodges's book *Harmony with God* only covers the New Testament. Though it is short and does not deal with the Old Testament or church history or objections, it is, in my opinion, outstanding. Indeed, it was Hodges's writings that led me to change my view on repentance.) For example, Mark Boda's *'Return to Me': A Biblical Theology of Repentance*,[1] barely covers the New Testament teaching on repentance. Boda has ten chapters and 125 pages on repentance in the Old Testament. He only has two chapters and 28 pages on repentance in the New Testament.

Similarly, David Lambert's *How Repentance Became Biblical: Judaism, Christianity, & The Interpretation of Scripture*,[2] emphasizes the Old Testament (as well as Pseudepigrapha and Rabbinic Literature) over the New Testament. Lambert's Primary Source Index has six pages of OT references, one page of NT references, and one page of Rabbinic references.

My outline reverses the emphases of Boda and Lambert, with ten chapters on repentance in the New Testament and one on repentance

---

[1] Mark Boda, *'Return to Me': A Biblical Theology of Repentance* (Downers Grove, IL: InterVarsity, 2015).
[2] David A. Lambert, *How Repentance Became Biblical: Judaism, Christianity, and the Interpretation of Scripture* (New York, NY: Oxford University Press, 2015).

in the Old Testament. It also includes chapters on repentance in church history, repentance and John's Gospel, and the preaching of repentance and salvation.

CHAPTER 1

Why Study Repentance?

Because Repentance Occurs Often in "Salvific Contexts"

REPENTANCE IS FOUND IN contexts dealing with gaining *salvation*, with receiving the gift of the Holy Spirit, with believing the gospel of the kingdom, with avoidance of perishing, with the kingdom of heaven being at hand, and so on.

While we must take care in each context to determine what is in view, it is easy to see why most Evangelicals think that repentance is one of the conditions of everlasting life.

In this book we will discuss the uses of *repent* (*metanoia*) and *repentance* (*metanoeō*) in the New Testament which appear to teach that repentance is required to be born again. We will evaluate whether repentance is indeed a condition.

There are ten passages which are most often cited as showing that repentance is necessary for salvation from eternal condemnation:

1. Peter implied in 2 Peter 3:9 that repentance is the way to avoid perishing.
2. The Lord said in Luke 13:3-5, "unless you repent, you will all likewise perish."
3. Peter in his Pentecost sermon said that repentance must occur before the Holy Spirit will be received (Acts 2:38).
4. John the Baptist and the Lord Jesus both proclaimed, "Repent, for the kingdom of heaven is at hand" (Matt 3:2; 4:17).

5. The Lord Jesus linked repentance and believing the gospel: "The time is fulfilled, and the kingdom of God is at hand. Repent, and believe in the gospel" (Mark 1:15).
6. The Lord's Great Commission in Luke linked repentance and the forgiveness of sins (Luke 24:47).
7. Paul linked repentance and salvation: "For godly sorrow produces repentance leading to salvation" (2 Cor 7:10).
8. Paul indicated what the believers in Macedonia and Achaia said about the believers in Thessalonica: "For they themselves declare concerning us what manner of entry we had to you, and how you turned to God from idols to serve the living and true God" (1 Thess 1:9).
9. Jesus told an account about a rich man and Lazarus, a poor man (Luke 16:19-31). They both die, but the rich man is in torment in Sheol, whereas Lazarus is next to Abraham in Paradise. The rich man begs Abraham to send Lazarus back from the dead to talk with his brothers so that they might repent and avoid his torment (Luke 16:30).
10. Peter was the first to take the message of life to the Gentiles (Acts 10–11). The Holy Spirit fell on Cornelius and his household as a result of the evangelistic message which Peter gave. Several Jewish believers who had gone with Peter to observe concluded, "Then God has also granted to the Gentiles repentance to life" (Acts 11:18).

We will devote a chapter to each of those ten passages, as well as one chapter to discuss various other texts which are sometimes cited (e.g., Acts 19:4; Rom 2:4; Heb 6:4-6).

Because Most Evangelicals Believe Repentance Is a Condition of Everlasting Life

It is not a stretch to say that over 90% of Evangelicals believe that repentance is a condition of everlasting life. Calvinists? Check. Arminians? Check. Catholics? Check. Orthodox? Check. The same is true for most Fundamentalists.

In this book we will look at quotes from leading scholars and pastors. We will evaluate their suggestion that repentance is required to have everlasting life.

Here is an example of a typical view on repentance and salvation by a leading Evangelical theologian, Dr. Wayne Grudem:

> The faith that justifies is never alone because it never occurs by itself, but is always accompanied by—or includes—repentance from sin and is always followed by other actions such as doing good works and continuing to believe."[1]

Grudem defines repentance as "a heartfelt sorrow for sin, a renouncing of it, and a sincere commitment to forsake it and [to] walk in obedience to Christ."[2] He says, "The gospel call, according to the New Testament, is ever and always a call to turn away from your sin as you turn toward the Lord to seek forgiveness from him."[3]

We will see many more quotes like these by several leading theologians and pastors.

Because Confusion over Salvation and Assurance Is Bad

If we get this subject wrong, it is bad.

If repentance is a condition of everlasting life and we do not believe and teach that it is, that is tragic. We are misleading others. And we may well have failed to do what is necessary to be born again.

If repentance is not a condition of everlasting life, and yet we believe and teach that it is, that too is a terrible error. We are misleading others, and we may not be born again ourselves. Does adding a requirement to everlasting life that is not actually a requirement mean one is not born again?

In this book we will consider these vital questions.

My challenge to you is to be like the Bereans of Acts 17:11. Be open to the Word of God. Whatever your view, be open to accepting what God has to say about repentance.

---

[1] Wayne Grudem, *Free Grace Theology: 5 Ways It Diminishes the Gospel* (Wheaton, IL: Crossway, 2016), p. 38.
[2] Ibid., p. 42.
[3] Ibid., p. 46.

People love to put salvation prayers in books. I don't, because I do not believe that there is such a thing as a sinner's prayer that results in the new birth. We will discuss the condition of everlasting life throughout the book. But it is not praying a prayer.

However, I will offer a prayer for insight:

> *Lord, please open your Word to my eyes. I want to understand, believe, and teach only what your Word says. Please protect me from error as I read this book about repentance. If there is truth in this book, then please reveal it to me through the work of your Holy Spirit.*

CHAPTER 2

Repentance in Church History

The Value of Church History

CHURCH HISTORY DOES NOT tell us what to believe. We must search the Scriptures to see what is true (Acts 17:11). We should not develop our theology based on the consensus of theologians.[1]

However, the pastors and theologians of the past have left us a legacy of interpretive options. Those who have gone before us over the past twenty centuries have given us a rich history of interpretations of Scripture.

The fact that various theologians from the past understood the relationship between salvation and repentance in a certain way does not mean they are correct. But they show us options.

While many Evangelicals think that all possible correct understandings are accessible in print, that is unlikely. Through theological libraries, we have access to over a million theological books. Yet those books do not contain every view ever held. Some views were either not recorded, or if they were, the books did not survive to the present day.

Frankly, I am not aware of anyone in print holding the view I advocate in this book until *The Marrow of Modern Divinity* was published in the UK (1645, 1649) resulting in the Marrow Controversy.[2]

---

[1] See Stephen R. Lewis, "Consensus Theology Taints Biblical Theology," *Journal of the Grace Evangelical Society* (Autumn 2010), pp. 25-39.
[2] See Michael D. Makidon, "The Marrow Controversy," *Journal of the Grace Evangelical Society* (Autumn 2003), pp. 65-77.

John Glas (1695-1773) and his disciple Robert Sandeman (1718-1771)[3] advocated salvation apart from repentance.[4] In his editor's introduction to the book on Sandemanianism by Andrew Fuller (1754-1815), Nathan Finn writes, "For Sandeman, repentance, or any other duty expected of a sinner alongside simple belief in the gospel, constituted a work and conflicted with the doctrine of justification by faith alone."[5] He added,

> As a Calvinist, Sandeman believed faith was a gift from God that was sovereignly bestowed upon the elect. He argued, "faith comes not by any human endeavors, or the use of any means even under the greatest advantages that men can enjoy, but of that sovereign good pleasure which provided the grand thing believed." Sandeman did emphasize the importance of repentance, but he steadfastly maintained it was the result of faith rather than an aspect of it.[6]

Three Hallmarks of Repentance Teaching in Church History

There are three main elements in repentance teaching throughout church history. First, repentance is understood as remorse over and turning away from one's sins. Second, repentance is a condition of everlasting life. Three, repentance is a key element in sanctification and for keeping (Arminians) or proving one has (Calvinists) salvation.

---

[3] See Michael D. Makidon, "From Perth to Pennsylvania: The Legacy of Robert Sandeman," *Journal of the Grace Evangelical Society* (Spring 2002), pp. 75-92.

[4] They did not believe that repentance was a condition of everlasting life. However, our views diverge in some ways. In contrast to me, they believed that faith is a gift of God and that repentance necessarily follows faith and is a key factor in sanctification. See Appendices 3 and 4 for my view on repentance and sanctification.

[5] *The Complete Works of Andrew Fuller,* Volume 9, *Apologetics Works 5: Strictures on Sandemanianism,* edited by Nathan Finn (Boston, MA: Walter de Gruyter, 2016), p. 8.

[6] Ibid. Luther's view, though different, is in some sense similar to that of Sandeman: "Although it is impossible to believe without repenting, as I have said above, when I proved that faith and grace are imparted amid a great spiritual upheaval; nevertheless, if this were possible, faith alone would be enough. For when God said: 'He that believeth shall be saved' (Mark 16:16), He did not offer His grace to repentance, nor to a work of any sort, but to faith" (Martin Luther, *What Luther Says: A Practical In-Home Anthology for the Active Christian,* edited by Ewald M. Plass [Saint Louis, MO: Concordia, 1959], p. 1213).

Repentance Is Turning from Sins

From the Apostolic Fathers to the present day, most people in Christendom have believed that repentance is remorse over and turning from one's sins.

The Westminster Confession of Faith says, "By it [repentance] a sinner...so grieves for, and hates his sins, *as to turn from them all unto God, purposing and endeavouring to walk with Him in all the ways of his commandments.*"[7] It adds, "Men ought not to content themselves with a general repentance, but it is every man's duty to endeavor to repent of his particular sins, particularly."[8]

Most theologians today agree. They understand repentance as turning from one's sins. The idea I argued in my dissertation, that repentance is a change of mind about Christ and thus a synonym for faith in Christ, is exceedingly rare. See Appendix 2 for more details.

Repentance Is a Condition of Everlasting Life

A system of works salvation emerged very early in the Church. Amazingly, the first generation after the Apostles distorted the good news which the Apostles had entrusted to their care. T. F. Torrance says concerning the theology of the Apostolic Fathers:

> Salvation is wrought, they thought, certainly by divine pardon but on the ground of repentance [self-amendment before God], not apparently on the ground of the death of Christ alone. There is no doubt about the fact that the early Church felt it was willing to go all the way to martyrdom, but it felt that it was in that way the Christian made saving appropriation of the Cross, rather than by faith...It was not seen that the whole of salvation is centered in the person and the death of Christ...Failure to apprehend the meaning of the Cross and to make it a saving article of faith is surely the clearest indication that a genuine doctrine of grace is absent.[9]

---

[7] The Westminster Confession of Faith, 15.2, emphasis added.
[8] Ibid., 15.5.
[9] Thomas F. Torrance, *The Doctrine of Grace in the Apostolic Fathers* (Grand Rapids, MI: Eerdmans, 1959), p. 138. For the opposing view see Nathan Busenitz, *Long Before Luther: Tracing the Heart of the Gospel from Christ to the Reformation* (Chicago, IL: Moody, 2017),

Augustine (AD 354-430) told the story of how he became a Christian by recounting a time when he wept over his sins and cried out to God. Then he heard a small voice say, "Pick it up; read it; pick it up; read it." He went to the bench he'd been at and read the first words he saw on the page, the words of Romans 13:13-14, "Not in rioting and drunkenness, not in chambering and wantonness, not in strife and envying, but put on the Lord Jesus Christ, and make no provision for the flesh to fulfill the lusts thereof." He wrote, "I wanted to read no further, nor did I need to. For instantly, as the sentence ended, there was infused in my heart something like the light of full certainty and all the gloom of doubt vanished away."[10]

Chapter 15 of the Westminster Confession of Faith is entitled, "Of Repentance unto Life." The first two points in that chapter say,

> 1) Repentance unto life is an evangelical grace, the doctrine whereof is to be preached by every minister of the Gospel, as well as that of faith in Christ. 2) By it, a sinner, out of the sight and sense not only of the danger, but also of the filthiness and odiousness of his sins, as contrary to the holy nature, and righteous law of God; and upon the apprehension of his mercy in Christ to such as are penitent, so grieves for, and hates his sins, as to turn from them all unto God, purposing and endeavouring [sic] to walk with Him in all the ways of his commandments.[11]

Jacobus Arminius, the father of Arminian theology, wrote, "God resolves to receive into favor those who repent and believe, and to save in Christ, on account of Christ, and through Christ, those who persevere [in faith], but to leave under sin and wrath those who are impenitent and unbelievers, and to condemn them as aliens from Christ."[12]

In his famous sermon, "The Scripture Way of Salvation," John Wesley clearly and repeatedly said we are justfied by faith alone:

---

pp. 169-90. I believe Busenitz is guilty of selectively quoting pre-Reformation authors. I find Torrance's work to be more credible.
[10] Quoted in Christina Andresen, "St. Augustine–A Model of Repentance." See https://www.ocf.net/st-augustine-repentance/. OCF stands for Orthodox Christian Fellowship.
[11] See https://reformed.org/documents/wcf_with_proofs/index.html?body=/documents/wcf_with_proofs/ch_XV.html.
[12] *The Works of James Arminius (1560-1609),* Volume 2, p. 465.

> Faith is the condition, and the only condition, of justification. It is the condition: none is justified but he that believes: without faith no man is justified. And it is the only condition: this alone is sufficient for justification. Every one that believes is justified, whatever else he has or has not. In other words: no man is justified till he believes; every man when he believes is justified.[13]

However, Wesley goes on to say that, in fact, repentance and even the good works that flow from repentance are also necessary:

> "But does not God command us to repent also Yea, and to 'bring forth fruits meet for repentance'—to cease, for instance, from doing evil, and learn to do well? And is not both the one and the other of the utmost necessity, insomuch that if we willingly neglect either, we cannot reasonably expect to be justified at all? But if this be so, how can it be said that faith is the only condition of justification"?
>
> God does undoubtedly command us both to repent, and to bring forth fruits meet for repentance; which if we willingly neglect, we cannot reasonably expect to be justified at all: therefore both repentance, and fruits meet for repentance, are, in some sense, necessary to justification. But they are not necessary in the *same sense* with faith, nor in the *same degree*.[14]

Wesley shows how confusing it is to argue for justification by faith alone and at the same time say that justification is by faith plus repentance.

In the Catechism of the Catholic Church, there is a section on "the sacrament of penance and reconciliation." It says, "It is called the *sacrament of conversion* because it makes sacramentally present Jesus' call to conversion, the first step in returning to the Father from whom one has strayed by sin. It is called the *sacrament of Penance*, since it consecrates the Christian sinner's personal and ecclesial steps of conversion, penance, and satisfaction. It is called the *sacrament of*

---

[13] John Wesley, "The Scripture Way of Salvation" (Sermon 43). See https://www.whdl.org/sites/default/files/publications/EN_John_Wesley_043_scripture_way_of_salvation_0.htm.
[14] Ibid.

confession, since the disclosure or confession of sins to a priest is an essential element of this sacrament."[15]

Well over 90% of gospel tracts and leading theologians today say that one must turn from his sins to be saved. Calvinist Wayne Grudem, for example, says, "The gospel call, according to the New Testament, is ever and always a call to turn away from your sin as you turn toward the Lord to seek forgiveness from him."[16] He also says, "Repentance from sin is a necessary part of saving faith," and "saving faith will include *a sincere resolve* to turn from sin and to begin a new pattern of obedience."[17]

Repentance Is a Key Element in Sanctification

Many today see repentance as vital to sanctification, and they see sanctification as a condition for gaining what they call *final salvation*. Others who see repentance as vital to sanctification do not see success in sanctification as required to spend eternity with the Lord. Both see repentance as vital in sanctification.

Roman Catholicism views penance as a sacrament and an essential element in sanctification. Within the Catholic viewpoint, ongoing sanctification is necessary to maintain one's salvation.

Though Churches of Christ do not call repentance *penance* and do not call it *a sacrament*, they do teach that lifelong repentance is required for sanctification and final salvation. At Christianity.com, under the heading "Churches of Christ believe in a process of salvation," the following six points are made:

> One must be properly taught, and hear (Romans 10:14-17);
> One must believe or have faith (Hebrews 11:6, Mark 16:16);
> *One must repent, which means turning from one's former lifestyle and choosing God's ways* (Acts 17:30);
> One must confess belief that Jesus is the son of God (Acts 8:36-37);
> One must be baptized in the name of Jesus Christ (Acts 2:38); and
> One must live faithfully as a Christian (1 Peter 2:9).[18]

---

[15] *Catechism of the Catholic Church* (New York, NY: Doubleday, 1995), Part 2, Section 2, Article 4, 1423-1424a, pp. 396-397.
[16] Wayne Grudem, *Free Grace Theology: 5 Ways It Diminishes the Gospel* (Wheaton, IL: Crossway, 2016), pp. 45-46.
[17] Ibid., pp. 70-71, emphasis his.
[18] Brannon Deibert, "Churches of Christ—10 Things to Know About Their History and Be-

After church-of-Christ.org lists hearing, believing, repenting, confessing, and being baptized, the reader is told, "At that point, the Bible says, you will be added to the Lord's church. But then, you must live faithfully for the rest of your life, and you'll find a home eternally, in heaven."[19]

Charles Stanley speaks for many Evangelicals today who do not believe that salvation can be lost, but who do believe that repentance is a vital part of sanctification, when he says,

> Confession means agreeing with God that what we did was wrong. But that alone will not keep us from repeating it. That's why repentance should always be a part of confession. We are called to live a sanctified life, one that is set apart for God and His purposes. Confession and repentance are an important part of sanctification.[20]

Conclusion

Church history overwhelmingly supports three ideas concerning repentance. Repentance is turning from one's sins, is a condition of everlasting life, and is a key aspect of sanctification. To determine whether those ideas are correct or not, we must turn to the Bible.

---

liefs." See https://www.christianity.com/church/denominations/churches-of-christ-10-things-to-know-about-their-history-and-beliefs.html, emphasis added.

[19] See "What Must I Do to Be Saved?" See www.beingsaved.org.

[20] Charles F. Stanley, "Repentance and Confession." See https://www.intouch.org/Read/Blog/repentance-and-confession. See Appendix 3 for the view that repentance is not a part of sanctification for the believer who is in fellowship with God.

CHAPTER 3

Repentance in the Old Testament

Introduction

THE ENGLISH WORD *REPENT* is only found ten times in Old Testament translations and one of those ten (Num 23:19) is a statement that God does not repent. In the remaining nine places, the underlying Hebrew word is *shuv* (or the noun *teshuvah*), which is most often translated as *turning*. The noun *repentance* is not found at all in most English translations of the Old Testament.[1]

So, the precise word *repent* is not found much in the Old Testament. However, the word *turn* (*shuv*) occurs over 1,000 times in the Hebrew Scriptures, often in contexts dealing with turning from sinful ways (sins, wickedness, wicked ways, etc.)

There are very few texts in the Old Testament which potentially show that repentance is a condition for everlasting life or the equivalent (being in the coming kingdom, having a new heart, being part of the resurrection of the just). Of course, a prime reason for this is that while there are many Hebrew words for salvation or deliverance in the Old Testament, they rarely if ever refer to regeneration. They always or almost always refer to temporal deliverance (from enemies, from physical death, from calamity, etc.).

---

[1] It is found once in the KJV (Hos 13:14), once in the NIV and NASB (Isa 30:15), three times in the NET Bible (Jer 31:9, 16; 50:4), and once in the CSB (Hos 14:2). It is not found at all in the NJKV, ESV, RSV.

Turn and Live (Ezekiel 3:19; 18:23, 32; 33:11)

Ezekiel has a number of verses which link turning from wickedness with living. These are sometimes cited as showing that the Old Testament taught that repentance is a condition for everlasting life. What do the contexts show?

You can easily see how the following verses could be used to teach that repentance is a condition for regeneration:

> "Yet, if you warn the wicked, and he does not turn from his wickedness, nor from his wicked way, he shall die in his iniquity; but you have delivered your soul" (Ezekiel 3:19).

> "'Do I have any pleasure at all that the wicked should die?' says the Lord GOD, 'and not that he should turn from his ways and live?'" (Ezekiel 18:23).

> "'For I have no pleasure in the death of one who dies,' says the Lord GOD. 'Therefore turn and live!'" (Ezekiel 18:32).

> "'As I live,' says the Lord GOD, 'I have no pleasure in the death of the wicked, but that the wicked turn from his way and live. Turn, turn from your evil ways! For why should you die, O house of Israel?'" (Ezekiel 33:11).

The most natural understanding of all these verses is that *physical death* is in view if the nation rebels against God. Is that not what we see in Leviticus 26 and Deuteronomy 28, the blessings and curses chapters? The wages of sin is death.

Charles Dyer comments:

> God was not saying that a saved Israelite would lose his [eternal] salvation if he fell into sin. Both the blessing and the judgment in view here are temporal, not eternal. The judgment was physical death (cf. vv 4, 20, 26), not eternal damnation.[2]

---
[2] Charles H. Dyer, "Ezekiel," in *The Bible Knowledge Commentary*, Old Testament Edition, edited by John Walvoord and Roy Zuck (Wheaton, IL: Victor Books, 1985), p. 1261,

Similarly, in introducing his discussion of Ezekiel 18, Charles Feinberg notes, "The subject of justification by faith should not be pressed into this chapter; it is not under discussion."[3] Later, commenting on verse 9 (which refers to life being conditioned upon obedience to the Law of Moses) he writes, "This statement, we must caution again, does not have eternal life in view, but life on earth. Eternal life is not obtained on the grounds mentioned in this portion of Scripture."[4]

Ezekiel 18 is not cited in the New Testament by the Lord or by any of the New Testament authors. Surely if these were key verses which show that repentance is a condition of everlasting life, then we'd see them used in evangelistic contexts by the Lord and His Apostles.

They Turned from Their Evil Ways (Jonah 3:5-10)

Nineveh was the largest city in terms of population in the world at the time of Jonah. If Jonah 4:11 is speaking of the entire population of the city,[5] then it was over 120,000. If it is speaking solely about small children, then the population was around 600,000.

The entire city repented. Men, women, and children. Even animals were covered with sackcloth and ashes. "The people of Nineveh believed God" (Jonah 3:5) about what Jonah had just said, "Yet forty days, and Nineveh shall be overthrown" (Jonah 3:4).

The king said in a proclamation, "let everyone turn from his evil way and from the violence that is in his hands. Who can tell if God will turn and relent, and turn away His fierce anger, so that we may not perish" (Jonah 3:8b-9).

Jonah says, "Then God saw their works, that they turned from their evil way; and God relented from the disaster that He had said He would bring upon them, and He did not do it" (Jonah 3:10).

While some might think that the king was trying to avoid the eternal condemnation of the Ninevites when he said, "so that we may not perish," that is contrary to the context. The issue is the overthrow of Nineveh (Jonah 3:4). That overthrow would have meant the death

---
[3] Charles Lee Feinberg, *The Prophecy of Ezekiel* (Chicago, IL: Moody Press, 1969), p. 99.
[4] Ibid., p. 101.
[5] Obviously, adults know their left hand from their right. However, some think Jonah might have been speaking figuratively here, suggesting that most of the Ninevites were childish and ignorant.

of at least all the men, including the king. He was hoping that their repentance would result in God's sparing their lives. And he was right.

Jonah 3:5-10 is alluded to by the Lord Jesus in Matthew 12:41, "The men of Nineveh will rise up in the judgment with this generation and condemn it, because they repented at the preaching of Jonah; and indeed a greater than Jonah is here." The Lord was saying that the people of Israel in His day should have turned from their wicked ways as a result of His preaching.

Was He implying that anyone who turned from his sins would have everlasting life? No. There is no hint of that. Compare John 3:14-18; 5:24; 6:28-29, 47; 11:25-27. In light of the context of Jonah 3, His point is related to the overthrow versus the sparing of Nineveh. Had the Ninevites not repented, they would have been overthrown. The nation of Israel did not repent, and so it was overthrown in AD 70. Over one million Jews died. Essentially the Lord was saying, "Forty years and the nation shall be overthrown."[6]

Let the Wicked Forsake His Way (Isaiah 55:7)

The Lord said through Isaiah, "Let the wicked forsake his way, and the unrighteous man his thoughts; let him return to the LORD, and He will have mercy on him; and to our God, for He will abundantly pardon" (Isa 55:7).

Because Isaiah 55:7 mentions God pardoning and having mercy on those who forsake their wicked ways, some see in this verse a suggestion that repentance is required for salvation from eternal condemnation.[7]

---

[6] In order for the kingdom to come for Israel, two things must happen: the nation has to repent, and it has to believe in Messiah Jesus. The nation did neither of those things in the first century. Only a small remnant believed and repented. But there is a coming day when the nation will be both repentant and believing (cf. Rom 11:26). At that time, the end of the Tribulation, the Lord will return and establish His kingdom.

[7] Under the heading "What Is the Gospel of Jesus Christ," I found this statement at a church website, "You must repent of all that dishonors God—Isaiah 55:7; Luke 9:23. You must believe in Christ as Lord and Savior, and be willing to follow Him—Romans 10:9. What keeps you from giving your life to Jesus right now? Repent and trust in Christ today." See http://langstaffassembly.com/the-gospel-1. Alfred Martin also implies this concerns eternal salvation in his commentary, *Isaiah: The Salvation of Jehovah* (Chicago, IL: Moody Press, 1956), p. 103. So also, John Martin, "Isaiah," in *The Bible Knowledge Commentary*, Old Testament Edition, pp. 1110-1111; *NIV Zondervan Study Bible* (Grand Rapids, MI: Zondervan, 2015), p. 1431, note on Isaiah 55:6-7.

However, two factors call that conclusion into question. First, the idea of receiving pardon is associated with temporal blessings and curses, whether individual (Num 30:5-13; Deut 29:19-20; 2 Kings 24:4; Ps 25:11; 103:3) or corporate (Exod 34:9; Num 14:19-20; 2 Chron 7:14; Amos 7:2), in the Old Testament.[8] Individual Jews who were away from God needed pardon and mercy whether they were eternally secure or not.[9] King David was born again when he committed adultery and murder yet he needed God's pardon and mercy (2 Sam 12:1-15; Psalm 51). Second, this text is primarily corporate, not individual. It fits within the Old Testament motif that God curses disobedience and blesses obedience in His people, Israel. This is a call for everyone in the nation of Israel to repent and to be blessed.[10] This chapter anticipates the coming kingdom when God will grant Israel *national salvation from her enemies and from temporal judgment*. Isaiah 55 ends with a glimpse of the coming millennial kingdom (vv 12-13). There is no indication that Isaiah is writing about what an individual had to do to have everlasting life.

Isaiah 55:7 is not quoted or alluded to in the New Testament.

Repentance Is a Condition for Escaping Temporal Judgment

The Old Testament makes it clear that repentance is a condition for escaping temporal judgment and premature death.

There is no reliable indication in the Old Testament that repentance is a condition for escaping eternal condemnation.

We now turn to the New Testament teaching on repentance and salvation.

---

[8] In fact, in the Old Testament pardon is never linked with justification before God or salvation from eternal condemnation.
[9] William MacDonald says concerning Isaiah 55:6-7, "The pathway of blessings lies in seeking the LORD and in forsaking sin" (*Believer's Bible Commentary*, Old Testament [Nashville, TN: Thomas Nelson Publishers, 1992], p. 982). J. Alec Motyer says, "*Pardon...is a word of general meaning: to do whatever must be done to deal with sin, a word focused on the fact of forgiveness without reference to reason or means*" (*Isaiah* [Downers Grove, IL: Inter-Varsity Press, 1999], p. 346.)
[10] While Isaiah speaks to individuals (e.g., "his way," "the unrighteous man," "let him return," and "He will have mercy on him"), he is calling upon everyone in Israel to heed this exhortation. National repentance is made up of the repentance of all the individuals of the nation (cf. Jonah 3:1-10; Matt 12:41; see also Matt 3:2; 4:17).

CHAPTER 4

The Meaning of Repentance in the New Testament

BEFORE WE BEGIN LOOKING at ten crucial New Testament texts which deal with repentance, we need to take a moment and discuss the meaning of repentance in the New Testament.

The way in which lexicographers determine the meaning of words is by studying their usage. For example, the *Oxford English Dictionary* (OED) was begun in 1857. It was finally completed in 1989 (second edition). It contained a whopping 20 volumes and 21,728 pages.

The OED editors asked scholars to submit the meaning of words *with an example of that usage in a work in that time period.* They had to provide a quote which used the word, the full bibliographic information, and a concise description of the meaning of the word in that citation. Each submission was on one piece of paper. There were millions of slips of paper which had to be collated.

We will first look at what the lexicographers have to say about the New Testament words translated as *repent, repentance,* and *turn.* Then we will look at some example texts in the New Testament, doing what the OED editors did for words used in English literature.

The noun and verb translated as *repentance* and *repent* are *metanoia* and *metanoeō*. They occur 55 times in the New Testament. Every major English translation renders those words as *repentance* and *repent.*

Under the only meaning for *metanoeō* with New Testament examples, the leading dictionary of New Testament Greek (BDAG) says it means "feel remorse, repent, be converted."[1] It lists 35 verses which carry this sense. Not a single verse is understood to refer to a generic

---
[1] BDAG, p. 64.

change of mind (or a specific change of mind about Christ). Concerning the noun, *metanoia*, BDAG says it means "repentance, turning about, conversion."[2] It lists 22 verses which carry this sense.

There are a few other words which relate to the New Testament teaching on repentance. These are the *-strephō* verbs. They translate the Old Testament word shuv in the LXX, and they refer to turning. They are sometimes used of *turning to the Lord* in the New Testament. For example, the angel told Zacharias that he would have a son (John the Baptist) in his old age and that his son "will turn many of the children of Israel to the Lord their God" (Luke 1:16).[3] Some of those references refer to turning to the Lord *in faith* (e.g., Acts 9:35; 15:19; 1 Pet 2:25). Others refer to turning from one's sins to (or back to) the Lord (e.g., Luke 22:32; Acts 3:26; Rom 11:26; Jas 5:20). BDAG lists four meanings of *epistrephō*, "to return to a point where one has been, turn around, go back," "to change direction, turn around," "to cause a person to change belief or course of conduct, with focus on the thing to which one turns," and "to change one's mind or course of action, for better or worse."[4]

The word *metamelomai* is used in the New Testament in the sense of "to have regrets about something, in the sense that one wishes it could be undone" and "to change one's mind about something, without focus on regret, change one's mind, have second thoughts."[5] It is not really a repentance word. Judas, for example, experienced regret (*metamelomai*) over having betrayed Jesus (Matt 27:3). He wished his action could be undone. But he did not repent (*metanoeō*).

While the lexicographers for BDAG sometimes inject their own theological biases in the definitions they provide,[6] the evidence suggests that they did not do so with these repentance words.

---

[2] Ibid.
[3] *Epistrephō* is also used in this way in Matthew 13:15; Mark 4:12; Luke 1:16, 17; 22:32 (of Peter after his three denials); Acts 3:19; 11:21; 15:19; 26:18, 20; 28:27; 2 Corinthians 3:16; 1 Thessalonians 1:9; James 5:19, 20; 1 Peter 2:25. *Apostrephō* has that sense in Acts 3:26; Romans 11:26.
[4] BDAG, p. 382. It suggests that *apostrephō* means "to turn something away from something, turn away," "to cause change in belief or behavior," "turn away from by rejecting," "to return something to its customary place," "turn back" (BDAG, pp. 122-23).
[5] BDAG, p. 639.
[6] For example, under *pisteuō*, believe, the revised edition, known as BDAG, added this curious statement: **"To entrust oneself to an entity in complete confidence, believe (in), trust** [emphasis theirs], *with implication of total commitment to the one who is trusted"* [emphasis added] (p. 817). The material in italics was not found in the earlier edition, known as BAGD.

The New Testament presents calls to repentance for individuals and for the nation of Israel. Usage shows that these are calls for people to decide to turn from their sins to the Lord. All who are away from God, which can include wayward believers, are called upon to repent so that they might escape temporal judgment (Luke 15:1-32; Acts 17:30; 2 Cor 7:10).

As discussed in the previous chapter, Matthew 12:41 shows that repentance is turning from sins. The Lord alluded to the repentance of the Ninevites in Jonah 3:5-10. The Lord said, "The men of Nineveh… repented at the preaching of Jonah." Jonah explains their response to his preaching in this way: "They turned from their evil way and God relented from the disaster that He had said He would bring upon them, and He did not do it" (Jonah 3:10). The Lord was implicitly defining repentance as "turning from one's evil way."

Some have argued (see Appendix 2) that repentance in the New Testament is sometimes a change of mind about Christ, not a decision to turn from one's sins. However, every New Testament use of *metanoia* and *metanoeō* refers to a decision to turn from one's sins.

Here are some example verses in the New Testament which use those words to show that repentance is turning from sins to escape temporal judgment:

> "Repent therefore of this your wickedness" (Acts 8:22).

> "I gave her time to repent of her sexual immorality" (Rev 2:21).

> "…unless they repent of their [immoral] deeds" (Rev 2:22).

> "But the rest of mankind…did not repent of the [idolatrous] works of their hands" (Rev 9:20).

> "And they did not repent of their murders or their sorceries or their sexual immorality or their thefts" (Rev 9:21).

> "They…did not repent of their deeds" (Rev 16:11).

There are no examples given of a New Testament text where *pisteuō* implies a total commitment to God. This material appears to have been added for theological reasons, not lexical ones. See Michael D. Makidon, "Soteriological Concerns with Bauer's Greek Lexicon," *Journal of the Grace Evangelical Society* (Autumn 2004), pp. 11-18.

It is true, of course, that the verb *metanoeō* sometimes appears in the New Testament with no stated object. When the text says, "repent therefore of this your wickedness," there is no question but that it is talking about turning from sins.

So, what about texts which have no stated object as in "Repent, for the kingdom of heaven is at hand"? There are two ways to determine meaning in contexts in which no specific object is stated. First, does the context provide some assistance? Second, does the meaning of the word elsewhere in the same book or the same author provide some help? While authors can use the same word in different ways, it is not uncommon for authors to use words in the same way in the same book.

Let's consider Matthew 3:2 and Matthew 4:17, which say, "Repent, for the kingdom of heaven is at hand."

Help in the immediate context is found in Matthew 3:3, "make His paths straight." That suggests that John the Baptist was to bring the nation back from its sinful practices to fellowship with the Lord. This is further supported by the fact that when John baptized people, they were "confessing their sins" (Matt 3:6).

In addition, the same word is used three other times in Matthew.

Matthew 11:20-21 is a rebuke by the Lord Jesus of cities in Israel which saw His mighty works yet "did not repent." He then says that if Tyre and Sidon, pagan cities, had seen such works, "they would have repented long ago in sackcloth and ashes." Of course, sackcloth and ashes were an Old Testament symbol of a decision to turn from one's sins.

Matthew 12:41 is a similar rebuke by Christ. He said the Ninevites, pagan Gentiles, "repented at the preaching of Jonah." When did the Ninevites put on sackcloth and ashes? See Jonah 3:5-10. It was after they were convinced Jonah was telling the truth that judgment was coming upon the city. Their belief that judgment was coming led them to repent in sackcloth and ashes.

The English words *repent* and *repentance*, when used in the New Testament, refer to a decision to turn from one's sins.

We are now in a position to examine ten crucial New Testament texts that use these words. We turn first to the call, "Repent, for the kingdom of heaven is at hand" (Matt 3:2; 4:17).

CHAPTER 5

Repent for the Kingdom of Heaven Is at Hand (Matthew 3:2; 4:17)

The Meaning of "the Kingdom of Heaven Is at Hand"

IT IS WIDELY THOUGHT by pastors and commentators that John the Baptist and Jesus were evangelizing when they said, "Repent for the kingdom of heaven is at hand."

Before I attended Dallas Theological Seminary (DTS), I was a quasi-Dispensationalist, though I did not know the term. I had read Hal Lindsey's *The Late Great Planet Earth*. I believed the Rapture was going to happen soon, followed by the Tribulation, the restoration of Israel, and the Millennium.

If you'd asked me before I went to DTS what "repent, for the kingdom of heaven is at hand" meant, I think I'd have had trouble explaining it.

However, I became a committed and, I think, consistent Dispensationalist during my seven years at DTS. Now I am not troubled by this question.

John the Baptist was Messiah's forerunner, prophesied in Malachi. He was to prepare the way for the nation to accept Messiah. Jesus is the Messiah, and He came to redeem mankind and to inaugurate the kingdom for Israel. But before the kingdom could come, two things had to happen to the nation. First, the nation had to repent, that is, it had to turn from its wicked ways (Lev 26:40-45; Deut 4:25-31; 30:1-10; Jer 3:12-18; 18:1-11; Matt 23:37-39).[1] Second, the nation had to believe

---

[1] See, for example, David R. Anderson, "The National Repentance of Israel," *Journal of the*

in Messiah for everlasting life (Gen 15:6; Jer 31:31-34; Zech 12:10; Matt 23:37-39; John 1:11-13; 8:54-59; Gal 6:16; Rev 7:1-8).[2] If both of those things happened on a national scale, then after His death and resurrection, Jesus would have returned after 3.5 or 7 years and would have begun the millennial kingdom in the first century.

"Repent, for the kingdom of heaven is at hand" essentially means, "Repent so that the kingdom may come for this generation." Of course, both Jesus and John the Baptist also taught the need for believing in Jesus Christ in order for the kingdom to come.

Commenting on Matthew 3:2, Alan McNeile says, "Jewish teachers were divided as to whether repentance was necessary for the coming of the Kingdom…but according to Matthew, the Baptist had no doubt about it, not as a means of bringing the Kingdom, but as a preparation for it."[3] Interestingly, McNeile distinguishes between what John the Baptist (Matt 3:2) and Jesus (Matt 4:17) meant by the exact same pronouncement: "But while both proclaim the near advent of the kingdom, with the one [JB] it was warning, with the other [Jesus] chiefly an *euangelion* [good news]."[4]

But the nation did not repent and did not believe. Hence the kingdom of heaven, which had been ready to begin, was postponed an indefinite amount of time. The kingdom remains imminent. It could have happened in any of the centuries up to the current one. Likely the kingdom will come in the twenty-first century. But we have no guarantee of that. See Chapter 14 and the discussion of 2 Peter 3:9.

Grace Evangelical Society (Autumn 1998), pp. 13-37; Michael J. Vlach, "Israel's Repentance and the Kingdom of God," *The Master's Seminary Journal* (Spring 2016), pp. 161-86.
[2] See "Will All Israel Be Saved in the End Times?" at gotquestions.org. Accessed March 19, 2019. See also John Piper, "Do Jews Have a Divine Right to the Promised Land?" at desiringgod.org. In Piper's case, he does foresee a future for national Israel, but only for "ethnic Israel," that is, Jews who believe in Messiah. He cites Acts 16:31 and Rom 3:29-30.
[3] Alan Hugh McNeile, *The Gospel According to St. Matthew* (Grand Rapids, MI: Baker Book House, 1980), p. 25.
[4] Ibid. Plummer also says regarding John the Baptist's message in Matthew 3:2, "The leading idea is that of warning: 'repent, for the judgment of impenitent sinners is at hand'" (Alfred Plummer, *An Exegetical Commentary on The Gospel According to St. Matthew* [Grand Rapids, MI: Baker, 1982], p. 27]).

Could Repentance Be a Condition for Individual Regeneration?

It is important to recognize that Matthew 3:2 and Matthew 4:17 say nothing about the condition for individual regeneration. They do not suggest that repentance is a condition for regeneration. But they do not deny it either.

Since the issue here is the coming of the kingdom for Israel, and not individual regeneration, we must look elsewhere (e.g., the Gospel of John) for that answer. But it would be a terrible mistake to conclude that "repent, for the kingdom of heaven is at hand" proves that repentance is a condition for everlasting life. It does not deal with that issue at all.

CHAPTER 6

Repent and Believe in the Gospel (Mark 1:14-15)

"Now after John was put in prison, Jesus came to Galilee, preaching the gospel of the kingdom of God, and saying, 'The time is fulfilled, and the kingdom of God is at hand. Repent, and believe in the gospel.'"

What Is *the Gospel* in Mark 1:14-15?

MANY PEOPLE SEE THE word *gospel* and assume this is talking about the gospel of 1 Corinthians 15:1-11. I know, because I took it that way in my doctoral dissertation.

That, however, is failing to note the context. No one had yet identified Jesus' coming death as good news. Indeed, the Lord had not taught about His coming death at this early point in His ministry.

The context is clear. Verse 14 explains what this good news message is: "Now after John was put in prison, Jesus came to Galilee, preaching the gospel of the kingdom of God."[1] Then in verse 15a, He makes it crystal clear what this gospel of the kingdom of God is: "The time is fulfilled, and the kingdom of God is at hand."

Though he does not fully adopt the view I am suggesting here, I. Howard Marshall comes close. He says, "the time of waiting and expectation (cf. Dan. 7.22) had ended and the kingdom of God had

---
[1] Some Greek manuscripts omit the words *tēs basileias, of the kingdom*. Thus, translations which follow the Critical Text, for example, NIV, NASB, HCSB, ESV, and NET, read "preaching the gospel of God." However, most manuscripts read "preaching the gospel of the kingdom of God."

drawn near. Here, 'kingdom' really means kingship or rule…Jesus summoned the Jews to repent in view of this great announcement. They as much as the Gentiles were not fit for God's rule."

William MacDonald sees this as "a bona fide offer of the kingdom to the nation of Israel…In order to be able to enter the kingdom, they [the nation] had to do an about-face regarding sin, and believe the good news concerning the Lord Jesus."[2] My only quibble with that statement is that they were to believe the good news *of the kingdom of God*, as verse 14 makes clear.

This gospel of the kingdom of God is not some special way that people were born again at that time. This was a message concerning national deliverance, not individual regeneration.

Believing the Gospel Means Believing the Kingdom Is Being Offered

The expression *the gospel of the kingdom of God* in Mark 1:14-15 means *the good news that the kingdom of God is at hand*. In other words, Jesus was saying that He had come to bring in the kingdom of God for that generation of Jews.[3] The kingdom could have come by AD 40. That it did not is because the nation did not repent and believe that the kingdom of God had drawn near.

The two conditions for the kingdom to come for Israel are national repentance and national faith in Messiah. While Mark 1:15 does not specifically speak of faith in Jesus as Messiah King, that is implicit. If the nation believed the kingdom was at hand in the ministry of Jesus, then they would believe in Him as Messiah King.

---

[2] William MacDonald, *Believer's Bible Commentary*, New Testament (Nashville, TN: Thomas Nelson, 1990), p. 136.
[3] I. Howard Marshall, *St. Mark* (Grand Rapids, MI: Eerdmans, 1967), p. 6. See also Barry Mershon, "Mark," *The Grace New Testament Commentary*, Vol. 1 (Denton, TX: Grace Evangelical Society, 2010), pp. 143-44.

Could Repentance Be a Condition for Individual Regeneration?

As in Matthew 3:2 and Matthew 4:17, the Lord's words in Mark 1:14-15 neither affirm nor deny that repentance is a condition for regeneration.

The issue here is the coming of the kingdom for Israel. Thus, we must look elsewhere (e.g., to Scriptures dealing with what one must do to have everlasting life or to be justified before God) to determine whether repentance is a condition for regeneration.[4]

---

[4] We will discuss the requirement for individual regeneration for Jews in Chapter 16 ("Repentance and the Gospel of John"). Individual regeneration is certainly required for specific Jewish people to be born again and to see the kingdom (John 3:3, 5). But for the kingdom to come, then the entire living adult population must be believers who are repentant (i.e., in fellowship with God). That will occur at the end of the Tribulation (Rom 11:26).

CHAPTER 7

Unless You Repent You Will All Likewise Perish (Luke 13:3, 5)

"I tell you, no; but unless you repent you will all likewise perish...I tell you, no; but unless you repent you will all likewise perish."

Two Examples Given of Jews Who Perished

I REMEMBER PROFESSOR HOWARD Hendricks at Dallas Theological Seminary stressing three words in our first-year Bible Study Methods course: *Observation*, *Interpretation*, and *Application*. Over and over again he said those three words and wrote them on the blackboard.

You cannot interpret correctly, Prof Hendricks would say, *unless you observe carefully*.

That principle is on prominent display in Luke 13:1-5. We cannot just pull words out and make them mean what we think they should mean. We determine what these words mean by what we observe in the context.

Two examples are given in this passage, one by the Lord Himself and one by His audience. These examples serve to illustrate what He means by the words *unless you repent you will all likewise perish*.

First, some told Jesus "about the Galileans whose blood Pilate had mingled with their sacrifices" (Luke 13:1). These Galileans *died* at the hand of Pilate.

Second, Jesus then brought up an example of His own: "Or those eighteen on whom the tower in Siloam fell and killed them, do you think that they were worse sinners than all other men who dwelt in Jerusalem?" (Luke 13:4).

Both examples refer to Jews who *died physically*. No doubt about it. Fail to notice that and you will misunderstand these verses as I did when I wrote my dissertation.

Likewise Suggests the Same Kind of Perishing

Twice the Lord Jesus said, "Unless you repent you will all *likewise* perish." Notice the little word *likewise*. It suggests that the Lord Jesus is warning them that they may be next. They may experience the same fate. That is, they too may be killed.

It would not make sense to say that these two cases in which Jews died physically illustrates that likewise unless you repent, you will be eternally condemned. Even so, many commentators understand Luke 13:1-5 in that way.[1] There is nothing about eternal condemnation in this context. The issue raised in verse 1 is why God allowed some Jews to be killed. That is the matter under discussion.

Jesus is saying that unless they repent, God will allow many more Jews to be killed, and soon.

All Refers Here to a Large Percentage

When I was working on my doctoral dissertation, my advisor, that is, my first reader, Zane Hodges, suggested that the issue here might be physical death. After all, over one million Jews died less than forty years later in the Jewish War of AD 66–70.

I balked at that suggestion because of the word *all*. However, I should have been more open to suggestion.

---

[1] See, for example, Darrell L. Bock, *A Theology of Luke and Acts* (Grand Rapids, MI: Zondervan, 2012), pp. 258, 264; C. Marvin Pate, *Luke* (Chicago, IL: Moody Press, 1995), p. 284, says verse 3 refers to "spiritual judgment before God, not necessarily a life shortened by tragedy" and that verse 5 possibly anticipates AD 70, but the words of verse 5 "more probably refer, once again, to judgment from God"; John Piper says, "Since Jesus connects it directly to sin and since he says it can be escaped by repentance, I take it to mean final judgment…Unless you repent, you too will be taken unawares and experience a horrible end—the judgment of God beyond the grave" (https://www.desiringgod.org/messages/unless-you-repent-you-will-all-likewise-perish).

The word *all* is often used in the New Testament to refer not to 100% of a city or nation, but to a large number or a large percentage. Here are two examples:

> *Matthew 2:3.* "Herod the king…was troubled, and *all Jerusalem with him*." There was widespread concern. But not every man, woman, and child was concerned. Many did not even know about the visit of the magi.

> *Matthew 3:5.* "Then Jerusalem, *all Judea, and all the region around the Jordan* went out to him [John the Baptist]…" Again, not every man, woman, and child went. But a large crowd from Jerusalem, Judea, and the region around the Jordan did go.[2]

Since the Nation Didn't Repent, Jerusalem Was Destroyed

It is easy to forget that Jesus is not only our High Priest and our coming King. He is also a prophet. While on earth He prophesied many things, including the destruction of the temple (Matt 24:1-2; Luke 19:43-44), which occurred in AD 70.

Jesus was prophesying in Luke 13:3, 5. He knew that the nation would not repent and that over one million would die. He warned of this in advance. Jonah only gave the Ninevites forty *days* (Jonah 3:4). The Lord Jesus gave the nation of Israel nearly forty *years*.

The coming of the Messiah for Israel was good news for that generation of Jews. But the nation had to repent and believe in Him to benefit from that good news. If the nation rejected Him and His message (John 1:11), then the kingdom would not come at that time. Instead, over one million Jews would die, and the nation would be overthrown and dispersed.

---

[2] See "Does 'All' Ever Mean 'All' in Scripture?" by Tom Hicks at https://www.biblestudytools.com/blogs/founders-ministries-blog/does-all-ever-mean-all-in-scripture.html.

Luke 13:1-5 Doesn't Tell Us What One Must Do to Have Everlasting Life

You do not need to be a Bible scholar to see that Luke 13:1-5 is not an evangelistic passage. The Lord says nothing about everlasting life or about escaping eternal condemnation. He does not call the people to faith in Him.

The issue in this passage is clear from the illustration the people bring to Jesus about the death of Jewish worshippers at the hands of Pilate. Why did God allow good Jews to be killed by Pilate? That was the question the Lord Jesus was answering. His enigmatic answer is that if those asking the question did not repent, they likewise would perish.

Jesus was not discussing the promise of life here. He was not even saying one way or another whether those who died at Pilate's hands or when the tower fell because they were in the spiritual far country (Luke 15:11-24). Regardless of why they died, the questioners needed to realize that they were in real peril of death themselves.

Leon Morris says, "His *likewise* can scarcely mean that they will be killed in exactly the same way."[3] Morris envisions two possible deaths. First, God might simply take their lives "in due course" as a result of their unrepentant sins. Second, "the point may be execution by the Romans. Unless the hearers repented, they would likewise suffer at the hands of the Romans."

---

[3] Leon Morris, *Luke: An Introduction and Commentary* (Grand Rapids, MI: Inter-Varsity Press, 1974, 1988), pp. 242-43. See also W. R. F. Browning, *Saint Luke* (London: SCM Press, 1960, 1965, 1972), p. 124, "The fact that Pilate killed some Galileans as they came bearing offerings to the Temple and the fact that eighteen men were killed when the tower of Siloam fell should be a warning to the whole nation, which is as guilty as those few."

CHAPTER 8

If One Goes to Them from the Dead, They Will Repent (Luke 16:19-31)

"There was a certain rich man who was clothed in purple and fine linen and fared sumptuously every day. But there was a certain beggar named Lazarus, full of sores, who was laid at his gate, desiring to be fed with the crumbs which fell from the rich man's table. Moreover the dogs came and licked his sores. So it was that the beggar died, and was carried by the angels to Abraham's bosom. The rich man also died and was buried. And being in torments in Hades, he lifted up his eyes and saw Abraham afar off, and Lazarus in his bosom.

"Then he cried and said, 'Father Abraham, have mercy on me, and send Lazarus that he may dip the tip of his finger in water and cool my tongue; for I am tormented in this flame.' But Abraham said, 'Son, remember that in your lifetime you received your good things, and likewise Lazarus evil things; but now he is comforted and you are tormented. And besides all this, between us and you there is a great gulf fixed, so that those who want to pass from here to you cannot, nor can those from there pass to us.'

"Then he said, 'I beg you therefore, father, that you would send him to my father's house, for I have five brothers, that he may testify to them, lest they also come to this place of torment.' Abraham said to him, 'They have Moses and the prophets; let them hear them.' And he said, 'No, father Abraham; but if one goes to them from the dead, they will repent.' But he said to him, 'If they do not hear Moses and the prophets, neither will they be persuaded though one rise from the dead.'"

The Location Is Hades, Not Heaven and Hell

Many people think that the rich man is in hell since he is in torment. However, it is more accurate to say that those in torment and those in joy are both in Sheol, the place of all dead until Jesus ascended to heaven.

We learn from this account what we always suspected: Hades (Sheol) had two compartments, one for the unsaved dead and one for the Old Testament saints. The believers were with Abraham. The unbelievers were in the place of torment.

As Abraham says, there is a chasm between the two compartments. Of course, we should not think that the separation is wide. The rich man is close enough to see Abraham and Lazarus. They are not miles away. They are close.

Of course, many think that this account is a parable. Maybe. However, it is not called a parable. And two proper names appear here: Lazarus and Abraham. Nothing which is called a parable has a proper name in it.

I think this actually happened. However, even if it is a parable, it is giving us accurate information about Hades (and about salvation too).

The Rich Man Thinks That Repentance Is the Condition to Escape Torment

Though the rich man is in torment, he is nonetheless able to carry on an intelligent conversation. In effect, he is debating with Abraham.

The rich man begs Abraham to send Lazarus back from the dead to talk with his brothers. He is convinced that if someone came back from the dead, then his brothers would repent and would escape torment.

Abraham corrects the rich man on both points.

First, even if someone came back from the dead, as Jesus would soon do, the rich man's brothers would not escape torment apart from faith in Christ: "If they do not hear Moses and the prophets, neither will they be persuaded though one rise from the dead" (Luke 16:31).

So the issue is believing the testimony about Jesus in Scripture, not additional miraculous signs.

Second, as seen in the quote from Jesus, the issue is not repentance. The issue is persuasion.

Abraham Clarifies That Persuasion Is the Condition

Twice Abraham refers to belief or persuasion. First he says, "They have Moses and the prophets; let them hear them" (Luke 16:29). To hear Moses and the prophets would be to believe what they wrote.

Then after the rich man indicates that what they really need is someone appearing to them from the dead who would lead them to repentance, Abraham said, "If they do not hear Moses and the prophets, neither will they be persuaded though one rise from the dead" (Luke 16:31).

Abraham repeatedly spoke of hearing and being persuaded. He was correcting the rich man.

Abraham Is Right, and the Rich Man Is Wrong

I find it ironic that many pastors and commentators think that the rich man, the unregenerate man, has a correct view of what one must do to have everlasting life. Instead of relying upon the words of Abraham, the friend of God, they rely on the words of an unbeliever in torment.

John Piper says, "But the question is, Will they [the brothers] be knocked out of their sins? Will they repent? Abraham says no. They will not repent. Why not? What will keep them from receiving Jesus for the financial radical that he really is? Answer: the love of money, the love of things."[1]

In a 2008 message on Luke 16:19-31, John MacArthur combines believing and repenting, saying that the rich man's brothers would have avoided eternal condemnation if they listened to Scripture: "Finally, they would have understood that they had to repent and believe. They would have understood the need for total abandonment, forsaking all other

---

[1] John Piper, "Preparing to Receive Christ: Hearing Moses and the Prophets." See https://www.desiringgod.org/messages/preparing-to-receive-christ-hearing-moses-and-the-prophets.

hopes, all other rights, all other gods, all sin and self-reliance, and have come to a true and living God."[2]

But Abraham said nothing about repentance. Abraham spoke about believing, not repenting.

Abraham is clearly speaking for and about the Lord Jesus Christ. The rich man represents the self-righteous teaching of the Pharisees.

Abraham is right. The sole condition of everlasting life is believing in Jesus. The rich man is wrong. Repentance is not the condition, or even a condition, of everlasting life.[3]

Darrell Bock accurately notes concerning this passage, "It was necessary to respond to Jesus with belief, since there is no other name under heaven by which it is necessary to be saved (Acts 4:12; cf. Luke 16:30-31)."[4]

Similarly, Robert Maddox comments on Abraham's words in Luke 16:29, 31, saying, "This last clause [v 31] has an unmistakable Christological reference, which recalls the more explicit Christology of the similar words in John 5:46ff., 'If you believed Moses you would believe me, for he wrote about me. If you do not believe his written words (*grammata*), how will you believe my spoken words (*rhēmata*)?'"[5]

---

[2] John MacArthur, "The Rich Man and Lazarus." See https://www.gty.org/library/sermons-library/CONF-RC08-10/the-rich-man-and-lazarus-2008-resolved-conference.
[3] Abraham does not explicitly say that repentance is not a condition of escaping eternal condemnation. However, that is a reasonable inference from the exchange.
[4] Darrell L. Bock, *A Theology of Luke and Acts* (Grand Rapids, MI: Zondervan, 2012), p. 140 (cf. p. 131). However, compare p. 264 where he says concerning Luke 16:30, "the discussion shows the centrality of repentance as an appropriate summary term for response." See also p. 363.
[5] Robert Maddox, *The Purpose of Luke-Acts* (Edinburgh: T. & T. Clark, 1982), p. 171.

CHAPTER 9

Repentance and Forgiveness Should Be Preached (Luke 24:47)

"And that repentance and remission of sins should be preached in His name to all nations, beginning at Jerusalem."

Forgiveness Is Not Everlasting Life

MANY PASTORS AND THEOLOGIANS suggest that the Lord is teaching in Luke 24:47 that repentance is the condition for everlasting life. For example, John Piper writes,

> Calling people to repentance is the reason Jesus came (Luke 5:32) and the message he commissions his followers to preach (Luke 24:47). It's the only way anyone can avoid God's judgment (Luke 13:3). Given the supremely serious consequences of not repenting, it's important to understand what repentance is.[1]

However, the Lord does not speak in Luke 24:47 about escaping eternal condemnation or about gaining everlasting life. He talks about the remission or forgiveness of sins. The word *aphesis*, translated as *remission* in the KJV, NKJV, and MEV, also means *forgiveness*, which is the translation of the NASB, CEB, NRSV, NIV, RSV, ESV, and NET.

---
[1] John Piper, "Unless You Stop Loving Sin: The Heart of Repentance." See https://www.desiringgod.org/articles/unless-you-stop-loving-sin. While by the words "God's judgment" Piper might mean *temporal judgment*, it is clear from this article that he understands the issue to be eternal condemnation. Indeed, the last section of his blog is entitled, "Repentance for Eternal Life."

Forgiveness is sometimes presented as a byproduct of regeneration by faith. Peter told Cornelius, "whoever believes in Him [Jesus] will receive remission of sins" (Acts 10:43; see also Acts 13:38-39)[2]. However, forgiveness in a fellowship sense is something which the born-again person regularly needs, as we discuss below.

Many have noted that John's Gospel only mentions the forgiveness of sins once, and that after Jesus' resurrection, in a non-evangelistic context (John 20:23; see also John 13:10, which figuratively refers to the forgiveness an already cleansed person needs). Never in John's Gospel does the Lord Jesus say that the one who believes in Him has the forgiveness of sins.

There are two major types of forgiveness in the New Testament: positional forgiveness and fellowship (or relational) forgiveness.[3] Positional forgiveness refers to a handful of passages which suggest that once someone believes, then all his sins, past, present, and future, are forgiven in terms of not being held against him. See, for example, Colossians 1:13-14 and Hebrews 10:17-18. Yet born-again people need fellowship forgiveness (John 13:10; 1 John 1:9; Acts 2:38; 22:16).

If the Lord Jesus were speaking of positional forgiveness in Luke 24:47, then He would have spoken of *faith and remission of sins*. Faith in Christ produces positional forgiveness. Repentance results in a lessening or cessation of temporal judgment (e.g., Jonah 3:5-10; Matt 12:41), but not positional forgiveness.

There is also another type of forgiveness. When at the cross the Lord Jesus said, "Father, forgive them, for they know not what they do," He was calling for forgiveness of *unbelievers who were guilty of bringing about His death on the cross*. This was neither positional forgiveness nor fellowship forgiveness. I call it *pinpoint forgiveness*, that is, forgiveness for one specific sin. The Lord was asking that the nation not be

---

[2] I think it likely that both texts are speaking of fellowship forgiveness. That is, Peter and Paul were saying that when a person believes in Jesus Christ, he starts the Christian life with a clean slate, in fellowship with God. However, even if both Acts 10:43 and Acts 13:38-39 refer to positional forgiveness of all sins, it does not change the fact that while forgiveness is sometimes presented as a result of the new birth, forgiveness is not the same as the new birth. Forgiveness is clearly a fellowship issue in some texts (e.g., John 13:9-11; 1 John 1:7-9).
[3] See, for example, "Positional and Relational Forgiveness, What Is the Basis?" See https://christianity.stackexchange.com/questions/46055/positional-and-relational-forgiveness-what-is-the-biblical-basis. See also, Kristopher Schaal, "Does the Bible Really Teach Two Types of Forgiveness?" See https://www.proclaimanddefend.org/2017/08/17/does-the-bible-really-teach-two-types-of-forgiveness/.

destroyed for its terrible sin. When Stephen was dying, he imitated the Lord's words at the cross, saying, "Lord, do not charge them *with this sin*" (Acts 7:60, emphasis added). The same sort of thing happened in Exodus 32 after the golden calf incident. The entire nation avoided destruction when Moses asked for their forgiveness, saying, "Yet now, if You will forgive their sin—but if not, I pray, blot me out of Your book which You have written" (Exod 32:32).

Fellowship forgiveness is likely in view in Luke 24:47. When we look at the Apostolic preaching in Acts where repentance and forgiveness are mentioned in the same context, *it is always directed to believers for fellowship forgiveness* (Acts 2:38; 8:22; 22:16). Whenever the Apostles evangelize in Acts, they are calling for faith in Christ in order to be saved (Acts 16:30-31; compare also Acts 10:43 and 11:14) or to be justified before God (Acts 13:38-39; 15:7-11). If they were commissioned to preach repentance for positional forgiveness, then Acts indicates that they did not obey that command.

This Great Commission verse in Luke is a call for the Apostles to preach repentance and forgiveness of sins not simply in Jerusalem and Israel, but "to all the nations,"[4] similar to all the Great Commission passages. An examination of the other Great Commission passages (Matt 28:18-20; Mark 16:15-16; John 20:21-23; Acts 1:6-8) shows that at least one is clearly not evangelistic (Matt 28:18-20, "go therefore and make disciples…baptizing them…teaching them to observe all things that I have commanded"); one is evangelistic (Mark 16:15, "preach the gospel to every creature"); and it is uncertain whether the other two are evangelistic or not. Thus, the fact that Luke 24:47 is a Great Commission verse does not imply that it is evangelistic.

Repentance Linked with Forgiveness, Not Life

The Lord said that it was necessary that repentance should be preached for the forgiveness of sins. In the next section, we will look at how the Apostles heeded that call.

Repentance in the Gospels, Acts, or epistles is not linked with everlasting life. Repentance is linked with the forgiveness of sins and with escaping temporal judgment.

---

[4] Bob Wilkin, "Preaching Repentance and the Forgiveness of Sins (Luke 24:47)." See https://faithalone.org/blog/preaching-repentance-and-the-forgiveness-of-sins-luke-2447/.

In Luke 17:3-4 the Lord spoke of forgiving your brother who sins against you if he repents. This is not salvific. This is interpersonal forgiveness.

In Acts 5:31, Peter said that God exalted Jesus, whom Israel killed, by raising Him up and causing Him to ascend to His right hand "to be Prince and Savior, to give repentance to Israel and forgiveness of sins." Here is another of the re-offers of the kingdom to that generation of Jews. If the nation had repented, God would have forgiven them, and they would also have come to faith in Messiah Jesus, and the kingdom would have come in that day. The issue is forgiveness and escaping temporal judgment. Of course, Israel did not repent, and the nation was kicked out of the Promised Land, and over one million Jews were killed (cf. Luke 13:3, 5).

After leading a group of over 3,000 Jews to faith in Christ on Pentecost, Peter called them to repent for the remission of sins (Acts 2:38). Since this verse is often confused as an evangelistic verse, we will consider it by itself in Chapter 10.

Mark 1:4 and Luke 3:3 report that John the Baptist preached "a baptism of repentance for the remission of sins." This was not his evangelistic message. This was a call for escaping temporal judgment, and it was a way to prepare the nation to be open to the preaching of Jesus.

John the Baptist's evangelistic message is seen in John 3:36: "He who believes in the Son has everlasting life; and he who does not believe in the Son shall not see life, but the wrath of God abides on him." See also John 1:7 and Acts 19:4.

The only other linkage of repentance and forgiveness in the New Testament is Acts 8:22. That is where Peter calls a new believer, Simon Magus, to repent of his wicked request and attitude that he might be forgiven in a fellowship sense.[5]

---

[5] For evidence that Simon Magus was born again (beyond the fact that inspired Scripture says, "Then Simon himself also believed; and when he was baptized he continued with Philip," Acts 8:13), see these four articles: https://faithalone.org/blog/simon-the-magician-was-born-again/; https://faithalone.org/magazine/y2001/01B3.html; https://faithalone.org/grace-in-focus-articles/salvation-the-sorcerer-acts-89-24/; and https://faithalone.org/journal/1989i/Inglis.html.

What We See in the Apostolic Preaching of Repentance in Acts

The words *repent* and *repentance* occur in ten verses in Acts. Above we discussed Acts 5:31; 8:22. In Chapters 10-11 we will discuss Acts 2:38 and 11:18.

Acts 3:19 is another re-offer of the kingdom to Israel. See the discussion of Acts 5:31 above.

John the Baptist's preaching of repentance to the nation is mentioned in Acts 13:24 and in Acts 19:4. This was not his evangelistic message, though it did sometimes lead to it, as Acts 19:4 shows ("saying to the people that they should believe on Him who would come after him, that is, on Christ Jesus").

Acts 17:30 is a general call for all men everywhere to repent. It was not Paul's evangelistic message. This was part of his pre-evangelistic message. When Luke reports the results, he says, "some men joined him [Paul] and believed..." (Acts 17:34). He does not say that *some men joined him and repented*. Evidently, they believed in Christ after they joined Paul and heard further teaching from him.[6]

Paul gives a summary of his three year preaching ministry in Ephesus ("repentance toward God and faith toward our Lord Jesus Christ"), pre-evangelism, evangelism, and discipleship, in Acts 20:21. We know from Paul's recorded preaching in Acts (e.g., Acts 13:38-39; 16:31; 19:1-2, 4, 8-9) and from his epistles (e.g., Gal 2:16; 3:6-14; Eph 2:8-9; 1 Tim 1:16), that he proclaimed justification and regeneration by faith in Christ, not by repentance.

Finally, in Acts 26:20 Paul reported how he called upon Jews and then upon Gentiles to "repent, turn to God, and do works befitting repentance." This was a summary of Paul's earlier ministry, not merely his earlier evangelistic ministry. If *turn to God* refers to believing in

---

[6] Paul does link the command to repent with the fact that God "has appointed a day on which He will judge the world in righteousness by the Man whom He has ordained" (Acts 17:31). Paul could not mean that all who repent will not come into judgment, because that would be contradicting the Lord Jesus Christ. In John 5:24 the Lord Jesus said that *the one who believes in Him* "shall not come into judgment" regarding his eternal destiny for he "has everlasting life" and "has passed from death into life." Repentance may well lead to faith in Christ. When someone repents, he becomes open to the teaching of God's Word, and by hearing it he can believe and be born again. Paul's point here was to grab the interest of his listeners concerning the Lord Jesus Christ, Savior and Judge, with the goal of their coming to faith in Christ. Some were interested, joined him, and believed.

Christ, which it sometimes does in Paul's words, then that refers to his evangelistic ministry. Two verses earlier, Luke tells us that Paul had said that Jesus told him to open the eyes of the Gentiles "in order *to turn them* from darkness to light, and from the power of Satan *to God*, that they may receive forgiveness of sins and an inheritance among those *who are sanctified by faith in Me*" (Acts 26:18, emphasis added). Compare Acts 14:15 (and Acts 15:19, the words of James at the Jerusalem Council).

Of course, the definitive chapter in Acts on the evangelistic message of the Apostles is Acts 15, the Jerusalem Council. There the words *repent* and *repentance* are not mentioned. However, *believing* (Acts 15:5, 7) and *faith* (15:9) are prominent. Hearts are purified "by faith" (Acts 15:9). Peter recounted his ministry to Cornelius and his household saying, "God chose among us, that by my mouth the Gentiles should hear the word of the gospel and believe" (Acts 15:7).

The Jerusalem Council confirms what was said above, that none of the ten references to repentance in Acts teaches that turning from sins is required to be born again. Of course, the Gospel of John and Paul's letter to Galatians confirm that as well. Those works do not mention repentance either, but they both clearly say that faith in Christ is the sole condition of justification and regeneration.

There is no hint in Luke 24:47 that the Apostles were to preach a different evangelistic message from the one they learned from the Lord Jesus (cf. John 3:14-18; 4:1-26; 5:24, 39-40; 6:35, 37, 39-40, 47; 11:25-27). And when we examine their evangelistic preaching in Acts, we see that they continued to proclaim the faith-alone message (Acts 10:43; 13:39; 15:7-11; 16:30-31; 17:4, 5, 12, 34; 18:8, 27; 26:18).

CHAPTER 10

Repent...and You Shall Receive the Gift of the Holy Spirit (Acts 2:38)

"Then Peter said to them, 'Repent, and let every one of you be baptized in the name of Jesus Christ for the remission of sins; and you shall receive the gift of the Holy Spirit.'"

Many Think Acts 2:38 Is an Evangelistic Appeal

YEARS AGO, I DEBATED a Church of Christ minister about what one must do to have everlasting life. Acts 2:38 was a verse he cited again and again. According to the Church of Christ, one must do five things to be born again: believe, obey, confess, repent, and be baptized. Acts 2:38 lists two of those five conditions.[1]

I find it surprising that many who do not believe in baptismal regeneration still consider Acts 2:38 to be an evangelistic verse. Most Evangelical commentators understand Peter in Acts 2:38 to be saying that the condition for the new birth is repentance.[2]

---

[1] In the debate, I brought out that there is no verse in the Bible which lists all five of the supposed steps one must take to be born again. This did not bother the Church of Christ minister. He said that God expects us to preach all of God's Word. I wondered too why the Lord Jesus left out four of the five steps (John 3:16; 5:24; 6:35, 47; 11:25-27). And why did the Apostles Peter and Paul leave out those same four steps (Acts 10:43; 13:38-39; 15:7-11; 16:31; Gal 2:16; Eph 2:8-9)? Why did the Lord and His Apostles all say that the only condition is faith in Christ? The Church of Christ minister said that in passages where faith is the only condition, the Lord expects us to understand that the words *faith* and *believe* include the other elements (obey, confess, repent, and be baptized). I found that argument to be specious.

[2] See, for example, I. Howard Marshall, *Acts* (Grand Rapids, MI: Eerdmans, 1980), pp. 80-81;

John Piper reflects the common understanding of Evangelical commentators. He suggests that while faith is not mentioned in Acts 2:38, faith is one of two conditions of the new birth, the other being repentance. He writes,

> "Well, verse 38 certainly could mean that [that baptism is a condition for everlasting life] when it says, 'Repent, and be baptized in the name of Jesus Christ for the forgiveness of your sins.' But it might also mean something like this: 'Receive the forgiveness of your sins by repenting and by believing in the name of Jesus Christ, which you signify through baptism.' That would mean that the name of Jesus and faith in that name is the essential means of receiving forgiveness, and baptism is the external expression of faith in the name of Jesus."[3]

Peter's Audience Came to Faith in Christ Before Acts 2:38

However, there is good reason to believe that Acts 2:38 is not an evangelistic appeal.

According to John 20:31 and 1 John 5:1, anyone who believes that Jesus is the Messiah, in the Johannine sense, has everlasting life and is born of God. Did Peter's Pentecost audience come to believe that? If so, when? Acts 2:37 indicates that the audience was afraid of being punished by God *for having crucified the Messiah*. That is, they believed what Peter said, *that Jesus is indeed the Messiah*. They came to faith before Peter answered their question with the words of Acts 2:38. Hence, they were born again before the words of Acts 2:38.[4]

F. F. Bruce, *Commentary on the Book of the Acts* (Grand Rapids, MI: Eerdmans, 1981), pp. 75-78; Charles C. Ryrie, *The Acts of the Apostles* (Chicago, IL: Moody Press, 1961), pp. 22-24, though he understands repentance as a change of mind about Jesus; William Barclay, *The Acts of the Apostles* (Philadelphia, PA: Westminster Press, 1953, 1955), pp. 23-25; Stanley D. Toussaint, s.v. "Acts" in *The Bible Knowledge Commentary*, New Testament Edition, edited by John F. Walvoord and Roy B. Zuck (NP: Victor Books, 1983), p. 359; Richard N. Longenecker, s.v. "The Acts of the Apostles" in *The Expositor's Bible Commentary*, Vol. 9 (John-Acts), Edited by Frank E. Gaebelein (Grand Rapids, MI: Zondervan, 1981), pp. 283-85; Darrell L. Bock, *A Theology of Luke and Acts* (Grand Rapids, MI: Zondervan, 2012), pp. 124-25.
[3] John Piper, "Repentance, Forgiveness, and the Gift of the Spirit." See https://www.desiringgod.org/messages/repentance-forgiveness-and-the-gift-of-the-spirit.
[4] A second proof is the fact that throughout Acts the sole condition of everlasting life is faith

Peter preached from the Old Testament, proving that Jesus is the Messiah. He ended his sermon saying, "Therefore let all the house of Israel know assuredly that God has made this Jesus, whom you crucified, both Lord and Christ [= Messiah]" (Acts 2:36).

The audience might have responded in a hostile manner to this preaching. They could have responded to Peter as a different audience later responded to Stephen, when they "cried out with a loud voice, stopped their ears, and ran at him with one accord…and stoned him" (Acts 7:57).

Those who killed Stephen were also "cut to the heart" at his preaching (Acts 7:54). In other words, in both cases the audience was moved by the message. However, in the case of Stephen, they gnashed their teeth at him (Acts 7:54), a sign of anger and hostility that led to them putting him to death.

In Acts 2 they were moved in a positive way by Peter's words. They did not cry out in a loud voice. They did not stop their ears. They did not attack Peter and take him out of the city and stone him to death.

Instead, Luke reports a very positive response by the audience: "Now when they heard this, they were cut to the heart, and said to Peter and the rest of the apostles, 'Men and brethren, what shall we do?'" (Acts 2:37). They believed Peter when he said that they had crucified the Messiah.

Acts 2:38 Is Answering a Forgiveness Question, Not a Regeneration Question

Peter's audience did not ask, "What shall we do *to be saved*?" (compare Acts 16:30). Instead, their intent was clearly, *what shall we do to escape our guilt since we now know we killed our Messiah?*

Peter's audience came to faith when Peter proved to them from Scripture that Jesus is indeed the promised Messiah who died for their sins and rose from the dead. Thus they were born again before their question in Acts 2:37 and before Peter's answer in Acts 2:38.

---

in Christ. See, for example, Acts 8:12-13; 10:43; 13:38-39; 15:7-11; 16:31. If Acts 2:37 does not indicate that they believed in Christ, then the audience was born again without faith in Christ, but by repenting and being baptized.

The Forgiveness of Sins and the Gift of the Holy Spirit Were Not Given at the Point of Faith Early in Acts

Even trained Bible scholars can misinterpret Scripture if they lose sight of the context.

It is true that starting with Acts 10 and the salvation of Cornelius and his household, both the forgiveness of sins and the reception of the Holy Spirit occurred at the moment of faith in Christ. However, prior to Acts 10, that was not the case.

The Apostles came to faith during the ministry of Jesus. Yet they did not receive the Spirit until Pentecost.

Paul was born again on the road to Damascus.[5] Yet he did not receive the forgiveness of sins and the Holy Spirit until three days later (Acts 9:17-18; 22:16).

Philip the Evangelist led many Samaritans to faith in Christ. Yet it wasn't until days later when Peter and John came and laid hands on the new Samaritan believers that they received the Holy Spirit (Acts 8:14-17).

In Acts, prior to the salvation of Cornelius and his household, people received the Spirit and the forgiveness of sins after repentance and baptism, not when they believed in Christ for everlasting life. Understanding the transitional nature of the Book of Acts is vital to understanding Acts 2:38. We now turn to consider that issue.

---

[5] In each of the three accounts of his Damascus road experience in Acts, Paul implies that he believed in Jesus: "so he, trembling and astonished, said, 'Lord, what do You want me to do?'" (Acts 9:6); "So I said, 'What shall I do, Lord?'" (Acts 22:10); and "So I said, 'Who are You, Lord?' And He said, 'I am Jesus, whom you are persecuting'" (Acts 26:15). In the Acts 26 recounting, Paul adds that the Lord specifically referred to the fact that Paul would open Jewish and Gentile eyes so that they may have "'an inheritance among those who are sanctified [set apart] *by faith in Me*'" (emphasis added). The final proof, however, is found in Galatians 1:11-12 where Paul says that "the gospel which was preached by me is not according to man. For I neither received it from man, nor was I taught it, but it came through the revelation of Jesus Christ." That rules out Ananias being the one who led Paul to faith three days after the Damascus road experience. If Ananias led him to faith, then Paul lied in Galatians 1:11-12.

Acts 2:38 Is a Call for Israeli Jews to Repent and to Be Baptized to Gain Forgiveness and the Spirit

Acts 2:38 sounds foreign to our ears. Why? Because this is not the message of John 3:16; 5:24; 6:47; 11:25-27; Acts 16:31; Ephesians 2:8-9; Revelation 22:17. It is a different message.

Once we recognize the transitional nature of the Book of Acts, the divinely intended understanding of Acts 2:38 should emerge.

Lanny Thomas Tanton was a Church of Christ minister who came to believe in eternal security. His newfound belief led him to Dallas Theological Seminary, where I met him. He wrote his thesis on Acts 2:38 and Acts 22:16. In 1990 he wrote two journal articles detailing the findings of his thesis.

Concerning his view of Acts 2:38—the same one I'm advocating—Tanton says,

> Because this view has not been widely circulated it has not been widely criticized. One work was found by a Churches of Christ debater which criticized this interpretation. However, its objections are of marginal worth because the polemical tone did not allow the transitional interpretation to be understood accurately. However, the chief objection (besides the objection that the view may be too complex) is found in the assumption that in Acts 2:37 some actually believed in Christ. This boils down, naturally, to the nature of faith and repentance (a subject beyond the scope of this paper).[6]

Philip's ministry in Samaria confirms Tanton's thesis. After leading many to faith in Christ, Philip baptized them (Acts 8:12-13). Days after they were born again, Peter and John arrived on the scene and "prayed for them that they might receive the Holy Spirit" (Acts 8:15). Luke adds, "For as yet He had fallen on none of them…Then they laid hands on them, and they received the Holy Spirit" (Acts 8:16-17). Prior to Acts 10:44-48, when Cornelius and his household came to faith in Christ, people did not receive the Holy Spirit when they believed in Christ. Acts 2:38 is best understood in light of the transitional nature of the Book of Acts.

---

[6] See Lanny Thomas Tanton, "The Gospel and Water Baptism: A Study of Acts 2:38," *Journal of the Grace Evangelical Society* (Spring 1990), pp. 51-52.

A careful reading of Acts shows that Acts 2:38 is not an evangelistic appeal to unbelievers, but an appeal to new believers to enter into a life of discipleship.

CHAPTER 11

God Has Granted the Gentiles Repentance to Life (Acts 11:18)

"When they heard these things they became silent; and they glorified God, saying, 'Then God has also[1] granted[2] to the Gentiles repentance to life[3].'"

Jewish Believers Grasp that Gentiles Are Now Part of the Body of Christ

WHATEVER "THOSE OF THE circumcision" (Acts 11:2) meant by what they said, they accept that Cornelius and his household are now part of the Body of Christ.

Did they understand that they are equal members of the Body of Christ? Probably. But a lifetime of prejudice against Gentiles would be hard to overcome in a day. See what Peter and Barnabas did in Syrian Antioch (Gal 2:14-21).

---

[1] The word *also* connects the experience of Cornelius and his household with that of the Jewish believers in Judea. Whatever those who contended with Peter meant about the Gentiles concerning repentance and life, they believed the same was true for Jews as well.

[2] Calvinists sometimes use this verse to prove that repentance is a gift of God. Of course, Calvinists think that saving faith is also God's gift (that is the way they understand the word *that* in Eph 2:8-9). However, all that is being said in Acts 11:18 is that God has allowed Gentiles the opportunity to repent. When Congress granted women the right to vote, it did not mean that all women automatically vote. It means that all women are free to vote if they wish. Acts 11:18 does not mean that God caused Cornelius and his household to repent.

[3] *Repentance to life* (*tēn metanoian...eis zōēn*) means *repentance resulting in life* or *repentance with a view to life*. The word *life* could refer to everlasting life or to physical life. Therefore, this could be a statement about what leads to everlasting life or something which leads to an abundant physical life.

Three Options on What They Believe about Repentance to Life

Those who contended with Peter are drawing a conclusion from what Peter has said. But what are they saying about repentance and life? There are three main options.

Option 1: Repentance Can Lead to Everlasting Life.

In this view they were not suggesting that repentance is a condition of everlasting life. They knew that only faith in Christ is. But they believed that repentance can and often does precede faith in Christ. A person who repents may start praying, reading the Bible, going to church, and talking with Christians. While none of those things are conditions of everlasting life, they can lead to the person hearing the saving message, believing it, and being born again.

Option 2: Repentance Is a Condition of Everlasting Life.

Unlike the first view, this view understands these Jewish believers as saying that repentance is a condition of everlasting life.

Some who hold this view say that these Jewish believers understood repentance to be a synonym for faith in Christ. So to repent is the same as to believe in Jesus for everlasting life.

Others who hold this view say that these Jewish believers understood repentance as a second condition, along with faith, for everlasting life.

Option 3: Repentance Is a Condition of Enhanced Physical Life.

The third option is that these Jewish believers were not saying anything about what one must do to have everlasting life. They were extrapolating from the incident they heard Peter explain. He had said that a group of Gentiles heard his message, believed, were born again, and immediately received the Spirit. They conclude that God has granted to Gentiles repentance that leads to *fullness of life*.

Were Those Contending with Peter Believers?

Those who had gone with Peter from Joppa to the house of Cornelius were believers. Luke says so: "And those of the circumcision who believed were astonished..." (Acts 10:45).

However, when Peter went up to Jerusalem, he was confronted by "those of the circumcision" (Acts 11:2). He does not say "those of the circumcision *who believed*." This omission may imply that they were unbelievers (compare Acts 15:1 and Acts 15:5).

However, in Acts 11:1 Luke says, "Now the apostles and brethren who were in Judea..." Those contending with Peter in Acts 11:2 might be *brethren*.

The contention in Acts 11:2 is far different from the one in Acts 15:1. In Acts 15:1, the objection concerned salvation: "Unless you are circumcised according to the custom of Moses, you cannot be saved." That is the position of the Judaizers (cf. Gal 2:3-5; 3:9-11; 5:2-4, 7-12; 6:12-15). However, the objection in Acts 11:2 concerns table fellowship, not salvation: "You went in to uncircumcised men and ate with them!" (Acts 11:3). That is like the objection of believing Pharisees in Acts 15:5, "But some of the sect of the Pharisees who believed rose up, saying, 'It is necessary to circumcise them, and to command them to keep the law of Moses.'"

Before Luke reports on what they said about repentance, he indicates that after they heard Peter's report, "they glorified God' (Acts 11:18a). They did not argue with Peter. They accepted his report, which was a faith-alone report.

It seems Luke is identifying those confronting Peter as Jewish believers who thought that Gentile believers had to be circumcised as part of their sanctification. But Peter has convinced them that no additional step beyond faith in Jesus Christ is needed in order to enjoy table fellowship with Gentiles.

Most Likely They Did Not Mean that Repentance Is a Condition of Everlasting Life

If those contending with Peter were unbelieving Jews, then they were likely arguing that turning from sins and law keeping are conditions of everlasting life. And if that was their meaning, then they were wrong.

However, wouldn't Peter (or Luke) have corrected them if what they said was wrong?[4] For that reason, and the reasons given above, most likely those contending were believing Jews.

In that case options 1 and 3 are possible.

Possibly those who contended with Peter decided that the Gentiles had repented sometime before Peter arrived and that their repentance had made them receptive to the message of life which Peter proclaimed (option 1). They were born again by faith in Christ. But their earlier repentance led them to be open to coming to faith.

Or, they might mean that these new Gentile believers are now in position to experience fullness of life if they repent.

Since we do not have any explanation by the people themselves or by Luke about what they meant, we cannot be sure.[5]

When Peter Recounts This Incident, He Mentions Faith, Not Repentance (Acts 15:7-11)

Many who discuss Acts 11:18 fail to see what Peter said about this incident. Luke does not tell us what he said *when he heard the words reported in Acts 11:18*. But Luke does give us his later statement.

At the Jerusalem Council (Acts 15), Peter reports on his ministry to Cornelius and his household. In his account, he mentions faith or believing twice. He does not mention repentance at all:

> And when there had been much dispute, Peter rose up and said to them: "Men and brethren, you know that a good while ago God chose among us, that by my mouth the Gentiles should hear the word of the gospel *and believe*. So God, who knows the heart, acknowledged them by giving them the Holy Spirit, just as He did to us, and made no distinction between us and them, *purifying their hearts by faith*. Now therefore, why do you test God by putting a yoke on the neck of the disciples which neither our fathers nor we were able to bear? But we *believe* that

---

[4] Of course, if the change of mind view of repentance is correct (see Appendix 2), then what they meant was that God had allowed Gentiles to change their minds about Christ (i.e., believe in Him) so that they could have everlasting life.

[5] The lack of details given in Acts 11:18 argues strongly against its being a key text explaining the relationship between repentance and salvation.

through the grace of the Lord Jesus Christ we shall be saved in the same manner as they" (Acts 15:7–11, emphasis added).

Conclusion: Acts 11:18 Is Consistent with the Faith-Alone Message

A comparison of Acts 15:7-11 with Acts 10:43 shows that Peter believed and taught that the sole condition of everlasting life or justification is faith in Christ. He never taught that repentance is the condition of everlasting life. And Peter does not correct the concluding comment made by those of the circumcision who contended with him (Acts 11:18). Therefore, it is highly likely that whatever they meant was consistent with Peter's faith-alone message.[6]

Therefore, Acts 11:18 is either a statement that repentance often leads to faith and everlasting life, or that repentance is a means to fullness of life.

---

[6] It is possible, of course, that the men made a false statement in Acts 11:18. They might have meant that repentance is a condition of everlasting life. The Bible reports what was said, even if what was said was in error (e.g., Gen 3:4, "Then the serpent said to the woman, 'You will not surely die'"). However, when a falsehood is recorded in Scripture, the context lets us know that it is not correct. That is not the case in Acts 11:18.

CHAPTER 12

Godly Sorrow Produces Repentance Leading to Salvation (2 Corinthians 7:10)

"For godly sorrow produces repentance leading to salvation, not to be regretted; but the sorrow of the world produces death."

Paul Is Speaking of the Repentance and Deliverance of Believers

I NOW FIND IT hard to understand how I ever thought that this verse was saying that repentance is a condition for everlasting life. I believe it was because I failed to look carefully at the context.

Yes, the word *repentance* is given as something which leads to, or produces, salvation. However, the *salvation* in this context is not the salvation of unbelievers from eternal condemnation.

The context is addressing a previous letter Paul had written which "made you sorry" (2 Cor 7:8). Evidently Paul is referring to one of two letters to the Corinthians that are now lost. It must have been a strong rebuke. It grieved Paul to write it (2 Cor 2:4-5). And it grieved the church to read it (2 Cor 7:8-10). It is clear that Paul is discussing the repentance of the church, born-again people, which had been complacent and had not exercised church discipline. But after getting Paul's letter, the church disciplined the sinning brother (1 Corinthians 5), and he evidently repented (2 Cor 2:6-11).

Philip Edgcumbe Hughes says concerning 2 Corinthians 7:10, "As Calvin points out, the Apostle is not commending repentance as though it were the ground of salvation—which would amount to a most un-Pauline doctrine of justification by works."[1] He then adds this comment: "In the case of the members of the Corinthian church, the nature of their response to Paul's letter was in itself a sure indication that they were, as they professed to be, genuine Christians, and not dissemblers." While we might challenge the explanation that Paul was suggesting their repentance proves them to be "genuine Christians," Hughes rightly sees that Paul is talking about the repentance of born-again people.

While the *New Geneva Study Bible* believes that repentance is a co-condition of everlasting life, it does not believe that Paul is talking about that here. It suggests that Paul was talking about believers turning from sins:

> *7:10 repentance.* Turning from sin, a sincere decision to forsake a specific sin (or sins) and begin to obey God. Here, the term does not specifically refer to initial repentance that must accompany true saving faith (Mark 1:15; Acts 3:19; 17:30; 26:20), but to a turning from sin in the life of a Christian.[2]

The church (or at least most in the church) repented of its complacency and disciplined the sinning brother. In turn, the sinning believer repented and was restored to fellowship.

Deliverance from Temporal Judgment Is in View

Notice that Paul speaks of two kinds of sorrow: godly sorrow and worldly sorrow. Worldly sorrow "produces death." Paul is speaking of temporal judgment and ultimately physical death here.

Godly sorrow produces the opposite. Instead of death, it produces life. When a believer repents, he is delivered from increased temporal judgment, and the result is that his life improves. The contrasts here are between worldly sorrow and its associate, death, and godly sorrow and its associate, life.

---

[1] Philip Edgcumbe Hughes, *The Second Epistle to the Corinthians*, NICNT (Grand Rapids, MI: Eerdmans, 1962), p. 272.
[2] *New Geneva Study Bible* (Nashville, TN: Thomas Nelson Publishers, 1995), p. 1837, emphasis theirs.

The Condition of Everlasting Life Is Not Being Discussed

Paul spoke of faith in Christ for everlasting life (or justification before God) in his preaching ministry in Acts 13:46, 48 and Acts 16:31 and in his writing ministry in Romans 3:21-31; Galatians 2:16; Ephesians 2:5, 8; 1 Timothy 1:16; and Titus 1:2; 3:7. He never once spoke or wrote of repentance for everlasting life.

Many commentators have noted that repentance is noticeably rare in Paul's writings. Entire books like Galatians, Ephesians, Philippians, Colossians, and 1 Corinthians have not a single reference to it. Romans has but one mention, and that not in a salvific context (Rom 2:4). Second Corinthians has two references to repentance, this context (2 Cor 7:9, 10) and 12:21, in which Paul expresses a desire that many in the church repent before his next visit.

If a Believer Falls, Deliverance Only Comes if Godly Sorrow Produces Repentance

Paul's teaching here is consistent with the Lord's three parables of Luke 15. Especially in the Parable of the Prodigal Son, we see a believer who falls and then later comes to his senses. He experiences famine, pain, suffering, and want. Those consequences lead him to repent (Luke 15:17, "when he came to himself"). He returns to his father and then experiences the joy and abundance of life which he lost when he went into the spiritual far country.

In 2 Corinthians 7:10, Paul is rejoicing that the church in Corinth repented and was restored to joy and put back on the path that leads to fullness of life.

CHAPTER 13

Turning to God from Idols
(1 Thessalonians 1:9)

"For they themselves declare concerning us what manner of entry we had to you, and how you turned to God from idols to serve the living and true God..."

Why Was Paul Giving This Report about the Thessalonians?

IN HIS FIRST LETTER to the Thessalonians, Paul never evangelizes his readers. He states on multiple occasions and in multiple ways that they are born-again people (e.g., 1:3, 6-7, 10; 2:7, 8, 10, 11, 12, 13, 17; 3:2, 6, 7, 8, 10; 4:13, 15, 17, 18; 5:1, 4, 5, 9, 10, 11, 12, 23, 25). He refers to "your faith" six times (1:8; 3:2, 5, 6, 7, 10). He calls them "brethren" fourteen times (1:4; 2:1, 9, 14, 17; 3:7; 4:1, 10, 13; 5;1, 4, 12, 14, 25). Twice he refers to "you who believe" (2:10, 13).

This is the letter in the Bible in which Paul gives the longest treatment of the Rapture (1 Thess 4:13-18). He is comforting his born-again readers regarding believing loved ones who have already died. They will not miss the Millennium. The dead in Christ will rise first.

First Thessalonians 1:9 falls within a section (1:2-10) in which Paul praises the believers in Thessalonica for the wonderful example they are to other believers in the area.

When they came to faith, the readers "became followers of us and of the Lord, having received the word in much affliction, with joy of the Holy Spirit." The result was "that you became examples to all in Macedonia and Achaia who believe." Unbelievers would not likely be examples to believers. Even carnal believers would not be examples to believers. Paul is commending them because they are exemplary brethren.

In verse 8, Paul rejoices that "the word of the Lord has sounded forth, not only in Macedonia and Achaia, but also in every place. Your faith toward God has gone out, so that we do not need to say anything."

Verse 9 continues from here: "For they themselves declare concerning us what manner of entry we had to you, and how you turned to God from idols to serve the living and true God." In other words, as Paul went forth in ministry, the spiritual health of the church in Thessalonica was well known and served to improve Paul's ministry.

The believers in Thessalonica did turn to God from idols. They were serving the living and true God. And, as Paul goes on to say in verse 10, they were "wait[ing] for His Son from heaven…"

Is the Concept of Repentance Present in 1 Thessalonians 1:9?

Turning (*epistrephō*) is often a repentance term. Turning to God from idols may be a statement about repentance. The reason I am not emphatic here is because Paul does not specifically say, though he implies,[1] that this turning to God from idols was something the Thessalonians did *after* they came to faith in Christ. If they had turned to God from idols *before* coming to faith, then it would be repentance.[2] But even then, it would not have been a condition of everlasting life but something the Thessalonians did in response to the preaching of God's Word.[3]

---

[1] In verse 8, Paul mentions the faith of the Thessalonians, which is before he says that they turned to God from idols to serve the living and true God. In addition, the sentence begun in verse 9 continues in verse 10 where Paul says, "and to wait for His Son from heaven…" The turning, serving, and waiting all are linked and are all things which would have resulted from new believers undergoing Christian instruction.

[2] A new believer begins the Christian life in fellowship with God (Acts 10:43; John 13:8-10). His life contains many sinful actions and thoughts which are for the most part unknown to him. The growth process reveals sins and leads to mind renewal and transformation of life (Rom 12:1-2; 2 Cor 3:18). But that is not called *repentance* in Scripture. That is growth, maturation, and transformation. So, I would not call this the repentance of believers, but the growth of believers. For a believer to have need of repentance, he must have departed from fellowship with God (Luke 15:11-24).

[3] Before coming to faith in Christ, a person might do many things to become a better person. See, for example, Cornelius, an unbeliever (Acts 11:14), whom Luke describes as a devout man who feared God and who prayed and gave alms regularly (Acts 10:1-8). Some think an

If this turning to God from idols is a report of what happened *after the Thessalonians came to faith*, then it would imply that repentance is not a condition of everlasting life.

That is Walvoord's view: "It was not reformation first and faith in Christ second, but it was faith in Christ first with the result that idols were forsaken."[4]

Paul's point is that formerly the believers in Thessalonica were serving idols, and now they were serving God and His Son, the Lord Jesus Christ.

Is the Context Salvific?

The context is a report about the spiritual health of the believers in Thessalonica. Paul's words include the fact that they came to faith in Christ. They "received the word" (1:6). Their "faith toward God" (1:8) had gone out so that the message of life was already known in many places Paul went.

So, while verse 9 is not describing what they did to be born again,[5] the overall context does include the fact that they came to faith.

---

unbeliever cannot turn from his sinful ways because he lacks the indwelling Holy Spirit. But the unbeliever still has the image of God within him. That image is marred, but not eliminated (1 Cor 11:7; Jas 3:9). See John Piper, "The Image of God," https://www.desiringgod.org/articles/the-image-of-god. Thus, an unbeliever can reform his life even before he is born again and indwelt by the Spirit.

[4] John F. Walvoord, *The Thessalonian Epistles* (Grand Rapids, MI: Zondervan, 1976), p. 16. See also Thomas L. Constable, "1 Thessalonians," pp. 692-93 in *The Bible Knowledge Commentary*, New Testament Edition (Grand Rapids, MI: Victor Books, 1983). However, though Constable says their turning to God from idols to serve God came after the readers were born again, he does call what they did *repentance* (p. 693).

[5] Contra Andy Johnson, *1 & 2 Thessalonians* (Grand Rapids, MI: Eerdmans, 2016) and D. Edmond Hiebert, *The Thessalonian Epistles* (Chicago, IL: Moody Press, 1971). Johnson says, "This [turning to God away from idols] is conversion language…Hence, what those outside are announcing is the audience's loyalty to the God of Israel, the concrete form of their 'turning to the living and true God to be saved'" (p. 53). Hiebert likewise says, "'How ye turned to God from idols' summarizes their conversion experience. The verb rendered 'ye turned' (*epestrepsate*) is the regular word for conversion in the New Testament and marks the radical change that has come into the lives of the Thessalonian believers" (p. 67).

So What Is Paul's Point in 1 Thessalonians 1:9?

His point is that he is proud of the believers in Thessalonica. The fact that they had turned to God from idols is a tremendous witness to their pagan, idol-worshipping, neighbors. It is also a tremendous encouragement to the surrounding believers who heard reports of what had happened in Thessalonica.

First Thessalonians 1:9 is not an evangelistic verse. It is nothing like John 3:16; 5:24; 6:47; Acts 16:31; and Revelation 22:17. If we wanted a parallel, we might look at passages which speak of churches which had done well. The church in Philadelphia, for example, was a faithful church (Rev 3:7-13) which had "kept [Jesus'] command to persevere" (Rev 3:10). Paul was very thankful for the church in Philippi, which was a partner with him (i.e., a financial supporter) in his gospel ministry (Phil 1:3-11).

It is encouraging that the believers in Thessalonica turned from idols to serve God and to wait expectantly for Christ's return. However, 1 Thessalonians 1:9 does not teach that turning from sins is a condition of everlasting life.

CHAPTER 14

God Wishes None to Perish but for All to Repent (2 Peter 3:9)

"The Lord is not slack concerning His promise, as some count slackness, but is longsuffering toward us, not willing that any should perish but that all should come to repentance."

We Should Not Assume That *Perish* in 2 Peter 3:9 Means What It Does in John 3:16

ELSEWHERE I HAVE ANALYZED every occurrence of the verb *apollumi* (*perish*) in the New Testament.[1] I showed that it refers to eternal condemnation less than 20% of the time. Normally it refers to some sort of loss or destruction, including physical death.

Apollumi in John 3:16 refers to eternal condemnation. The context makes that clear (see John 3:17-18). However, the context in 2 Peter 3:1-13 is radically different from John 3:14-18.

Perishing in 2 Peter 3:9 Refers to Premature Death, Not Eternal Condemnation

Peter says, "The Lord…is not willing that any should perish but that all should come to repentance." Most people see that as an

---

[1] See Robert N. Wilkin, *The Ten Most Misunderstood Words in the Bible* (N.P.: Grace Evangelical Society, 2012), pp. 53-69, esp. pp. 56-65.

obvious statement that repentance is the condition for escaping eternal condemnation.[2]

But the issue in 2 Peter 3:1-8 is the timing of "the promise of His coming." In verse 4 Peter says the mockers were saying, "Where is the promise of His coming?" A point often missed is verse 9 starts with the words, "The Lord is not slack concerning His promise [i.e., the promise of His coming]."

When Peter is writing, it is around AD 66, or 33 years after Jesus ascended to heaven with a promise to return. Though we may think that 33 years is not very long to wait, we must understand that the first century believers thought it likely that Jesus would return in their lifetimes (as we do in the twenty-first century).

Verse 9 explains why Jesus had delayed fulfilling His promise to return and establish His kingdom. Peter's readers knew that Christ's return will involve rapturing all believers off of earth, followed by seven years of Tribulation. Concerning those seven years, the Lord said, "For then there will be great tribulation, such as has not been since the beginning of the world until this time, no, nor ever shall be. And unless those days were shortened, no flesh would be saved, but for the elect's sake those days will be shortened" (Matt 24:21-22).

God is not longing for the tribulation. As long as enough people on earth repent, the tribulation will continue to be postponed.[3]

Repentance postpones His coming. It does not eliminate eternal condemnation. Peter made clear that the only way to escape eternal

---

[2] See, for example, Michael Green, *The Second Epistle of Peter and the Epistle of Jude* (Grand Rapids, MI: Eerdmans, 1968), pp. 135-36; J. N. D. Kelly, *A Commentary on the Epistles of Peter and Jude* (Grand Rapids, MI: Baker, 1969), pp. 362-63; Donald Senior, *1 & 2 Peter* (Wilmington, DE: Michael Glazier, Inc., 1980), pp. 134-35; Joseph B. Mayor, *The Epistles of Jude and II Peter* (Grand Rapids, MI: Baker, 1907, 1979), pp. 156-57; Kenneth O. Gangel, s.v., "2 Peter" in *The Bible Knowledge Commentary*, New Testament Edition, Edited by John F. Walvoord and Roy B. Zuck (NP: Victor Books, 1983), p. 876.

[3] One of my editors asked, "How many people are enough?" That is, how many people on earth at any given time need to repent (or need to continue in fellowship with Him) in order to forestall the Tribulation? That is a great question. We know from the Old Testament that nations fell when their national sins crossed some undefined tipping point. For example, "But in the fourth generation they shall return here, *for the iniquity of the Amorites is not yet complete*" (Gen 15:16, emphasis added). The flood, alluded to in 2 Peter 3:6, did not occur until the sins of mankind were full (cf. Gen 6:1-8). That was true for Israel as well (Leviticus 26). God did not give percentages then. Nor does He do so now.

condemnation is by believing in the Lord Jesus Christ (Acts 10:43; 15:7-11; 1 Pet 1:21-24).

The Context Concerns the Coming Tribulation and Billions of Deaths

A simple rule of hermeneutics is that you determine the meaning of a word by its use in context. Well, here it is obvious what *apollumi* means in context if we just read the words before and after verse nine. In verse six the same word is used to refer to those who died in the Noahic flood: "The world that then existed perished, being flooded with water." That's the only other use of this word in Second Peter and it is in the immediate context. (There is also one use of the word in First Peter and it also carries this meaning.)

In addition, verse nine is culminating a discussion begun in verses 3 and following about the delay in the Lord's promised return. Peter is saying in verse 9 that the Lord will fulfill His promise, but He is delaying since He is longsuffering toward us humans. He doesn't want to kill billions of people on earth. He would rather people repent and live full lives here and now prior to the kingdom. But when the sins of mankind are filled up, then the Tribulation will begin, and billions will die. Even then, however, God will show that He would prefer that men repent and avoid premature death (Rev 9:20-21; 16:9, 11).

The verses which follow 2 Peter 3:9, that is, verses 10-13, discuss not hell, but the destruction of the current earth and heavens by fire. Temporal destruction is what is being discussed. The ultimate end, of course, is that His promise will be fulfilled: we will receive "a new heavens and a new earth in which righteousness dwells" (verse 13).

Zane Hodges writes,

> What God seeks from men while His judgment tarries is repentance. God's wish, therefore, is that all should come to repentance. This statement should not be read as though it indicated God's desire that all men should be *saved from hell*. It is true that God *does* have such a desire, since it is plainly stated in 1 Tim 2:4-5 and also found in passages like John 3:16-17 and 2 Cor 5:19-20. What is suggested here, however, is that if men would repent, the judgment of the Day of the Lord could be

averted [i.e., postponed]. But this repentance would need to be universal, that is to say, *all* would have to *come to repentance*.

This truth is illustrated in microcosm in the case of Nineveh (Jonah 3)… What is clear is that *all of them* were spared from the impending "overthrow" of their city, because *the whole city* repented.[4]

Thus, we might paraphrase 2 Peter 3:9 in this way: God wishes that none should die prematurely under His hand of temporal judgment (especially during the calamitous judgments of the Tribulation), but that all should come to repentance and extend their lives and their experience of His blessings.

Of course, the longer the Church Age continues, the more generations of people have the opportunity to believe and be saved. The delay thus far has meant that many more generations have been born, and many more people have come to faith and been born again. Say the Lord had returned in AD 70. Hundreds of millions or even billions of people who have since been born again would not have been. So, delaying the return gives more people more opportunity to believe and be born again. While that is not explicitly mentioned in this passage, it is certainly something that Peter and the other Apostles believed and taught (cf. Acts 15:7-11; 1 Tim 2:4; 1 Pet 1:23-25).[5]

Second Peter 3:9 illustrates the truth of Ezekiel 18. Unrighteousness leads to premature death, and repentance is the remedy: "'Do I have any pleasure at all that the wicked should die?' says the Lord God, 'and not that he should turn from his ways and live?'" (Ezek 18:23).

---

[4] Zane C. Hodges, *Second Peter: Shunning Error in Light of the Savior's Return* (Denton, TX: Grace Evangelical Society, 2015), pp. 104-105.
[5] Charles Haddon Spurgeon made this comment about 2 Peter 3:9, "While I have prayed, 'Come quickly,' I have often felt inclined to contradict myself and cry, 'Yet tarry for a while, good Lord. Let mercy's day be lengthened. Let the heathen yet receive the Savior.' We may desire the coming of the Lord, but we ought also to be in sympathy with the tarrying of the Most High, to which his loving heart inclines him." Cited at https://www.preceptaustin.org/2_peter_devotionals.

CHAPTER 15

Other Verses Thought to Link Salvation and Repentance

Introduction

THUS FAR WE HAVE considered the ten texts which are most often cited as proving that repentance is a condition of everlasting life. Those texts are:

- Matthew 3:2 (and 4:17).
- Mark 1:14-15.
- Luke 13: 3, 5.
- Luke 16:19-31.
- Luke 24:47.
- Acts 2:38.
- Acts 11:18.
- 2 Corinthians 7:10.
- 1 Thessalonians 1:9.
- 2 Peter 3:9.

We now turn to a handful of other passages which are occasionally cited in an effort to prove that repentance is a condition of everlasting life. These will be combined in just one chapter, thus receiving less discussion, because they are widely recognized as not being primary passages on repentance.

Luke 15:7, 10

"I say to you that likewise there will be more joy in heaven over one sinner who repents than over ninety-nine just persons who need no repentance...Likewise, I say to you, there is joy in the presence of the angels of God over one sinner who repents."

Most commentators think that the rejoicing in heaven over one sinner who repents is rejoicing due to *unbelievers* repenting *and being born again*.[1] However, the Lord said that the lost sheep was once part of the group of one hundred just sheep which did not need to repent. Only after straying did it need to repent. The same with the lost coin. It was with the other nine coins until it was lost. The repentance of the lost sheep and the lost coin (and the lost son) illustrates believers in fellowship with God who stray and then repent, returning to fellowship. The issue is not eternal destiny, but fellowship with God.

Acts 17:30

"Truly, these times of ignorance God overlooked, but now commands all men everywhere to repent."

This is part of Paul's Mars Hill message in Athens. He was reaching out to pagan philosophers. He says that God commands all men everywhere to repent "because He has appointed a day on which He will judge the world in righteousness by the Man whom He has ordained" (Acts 17:31a). Paul then adds, "He has given assurance of this to all by raising Him from the dead" (Acts 17:31b). This is a rather oblique reference to Jesus. There is no mention of His name or His substitutionary death on the cross. Yet Paul's remarks did result in interest. Some joined Paul and learned more from him ("We will hear you again on this matter," verse 32), for verse 34 says, "However, some men joined him and believed..."

---

[1] See, for example, Darrell L. Bock, *A Theology of Luke and Acts* (Grand Rapids, MI: Zondervan, 2012), p. 264; C. Marvin Pate, *Luke* (Chicago, IL: Moody Press, 1995), pp. 302-304; John Piper, "Mission: The Gladness of God." See https://www.desiringgod.org/messages/mission-the-gladness-of-god.

Many commentators understand Paul to be saying that all who repent are saved from eternal condemnation.[2]

But before we conclude that this is an evangelistic message, we should ponder why Paul did not mention the name of Jesus, the cross, justification, salvation, everlasting life, or faith in Christ. Why are all those hallmarks of Paul's evangelistic ministry (cf. Acts 13:26-48; 16:31; see also Gal 2:16; Eph 2:8-9) missing here? Could he be doing something other than evangelism? It could be that he is trying to arouse interest so that he can evangelize those who respond positively to his pre-evangelistic message.

Paul was not saying that all who repent have everlasting life. Nowhere did he say or write that. Paul proclaimed salvation by grace *through faith*[3] apart from works (Acts 16:31; Rom 4:4-5; Gal 2:16; Eph 2:8-9). Al Valdes says,

> The repentance here refers to forsaking the polytheistic and idolatrous pagan notions of God and seeking a vital and real relationship with the true God. The message here mirrors what Paul and Barnabas exhorted the idolatrous worshippers at Lystra to do (cf. Acts 14:15). While this is not a condition of eternal life, the unbeliever who repents places himself in a proper sphere to understand the saving message (cf. v 27; 10:35).[4]

Richard Longenecker similarly says,

> In the person and work of Jesus, God has acted in such a manner as to make idolatry particularly heinous. To

---

[2] For examples of commentators who believe that Paul is saying that repentance is the condition of eternal salvation, see Bock, *A Theology of Luke and Acts*, pp. 117, 132; F. F. Bruce, *Commentary on the Book of Acts* (Grand Rapids, MI: Eerdmans, 1981), p. 361; I. Howard Marshall, *Acts* (Grand Rapids, MI: Eerdmans, 1980), p. 290.

[3] John Piper interprets Acts 17:30 to be an evangelistic text, saying, "The times of ignorance are over and God commands you to repent, believe in Jesus Christ, and be saved from the judgment of God." Paul did not mention believing in Jesus Christ. Nor did he mention being saved from the judgment of God, though that may be implied. Since Piper believes that faith in Christ is the condition for salvation, he supplies what Paul did not. But if Paul did not say that here, we should take that into account in our interpretation. See https://www.desiringgod.org/messages/the-age-of-ignorance-is-over.

[4] Al Valdes, s.v. "Acts" in *The Grace New Testament Commentary*, Volume 1, edited by Robert N. Wilkin (Denton, TX: Grace Evangelical Society, 2010), p. 574.

reject Jesus, therefore, is to reject the person and vicarious intervention of God on behalf of man and to open oneself up in the future to divine judgment metedced out by the very one rejected in the present. And God himself has authenticated all this by raising Jesus from the dead.[5]

Paul's point in mentioning repentance and eschatological judgment was to move the listeners away from idolatry (repentance in this context—see verse 29—concerns turning away from idolatry) to hear and believe the promise of life. Some did. It is noteworthy that when Luke gives a report on the results of Paul's preaching and subsequent ministry, he says, "However, some men joined him *and believed…*" (Acts 17:34, emphasis added). Luke did not say that *some men joined him and repented.*

Acts 20:21

"…testifying to Jews, and also to Greeks, repentance toward God and faith toward our Lord Jesus Christ."

While many think that Paul is stating the content *of his evangelistic message,*[6] it is more reasonable to see this as Paul's statement of the purpose *of his entire preaching ministry.* He preached to turn men from their sins and to God, and he called upon men to believe in the Lord Jesus Christ.

Romans 2:4

"Or do you despise the riches of His goodness, forbearance, and longsuffering, not knowing that the goodness of God leads you to repentance?"

---

[5] Richard N. Longenecker, s.v. "The Acts of the Apostles" in *The Expositor's Bible Commentary*, Volume 9 (Grand Rapids, MI: Zondervan, 1981), p. 477.
[6] See, for example, Bock, *A Theology of Luke and Acts*, p. 263; Bruce, *Acts*, p. 413; Marshall, *Acts*, p. 331.

I mention Romans 2:4 because it is the one and only reference to repentance in Paul's letter to the Romans.[7] When compared with Romans 3:21–4:25, where the sole condition of justification is faith in Christ, it is clear that Paul is not saying that repentance is a condition for justification or regeneration.[8] In Romans 2 Paul is writing to the moralist, the one who thinks he can be justified by his own works (Rom 2:1-3). In verse 4 Paul is saying the goodness of God should lead him to repentance. In this context, repentance would be a turning from his self-righteous attitudes and an openness to hear what God says one must do to be righteous before Him.

Hebrews 6:6

"…[For it is impossible…] if they fall away, to renew them again to repentance, since they crucify again for themselves the Son of God, and put Him to an open shame."

This warning is often understood as proof that some who initially responded positively toward Christ later fell away (apostatized) and proved that they were never born again.[9] Some, who also see the issue as eternal destiny, suggest that the author is warning about a *hypothetical situation* which would never really happen, where a believer apostatizes

---

[7] In all his epistles combined, Paul only uses the noun *metanoia* four times (Rom 2:4; 2 Cor 7:9, 10; 2 Tim 2:25) and the verb *metanoeō* once (2 Cor 12:21). Five uses total. He did not mention repentance at all in ten of his thirteen epistles. This fact led James D. G. Dunn to comment that repentance is "a category strikingly absent from Paul" ("The Justice of God: A Renewed Perspective on Justification by Faith," *Journal of Theological Studies*, New Series, 43 [April 1992]: 7).

[8] Many commentators, however, think that Paul is saying that repentance is a condition for justification. See John MacArthur, *The MacArthur New Testament Commentary: Romans 1-8* (Chicago, IL: Moody Publishers, 1991), pp. 120-21; C. E. B. Cranfield, *The Epistle to the Romans*, ICC Series, Vol. 1 (Edinburgh: T. & T. Clark, 1975), pp. 144-45, esp. note 2 ["repentance is for Paul an integral element of *pistis* (faith)"]; John Murray, *The Epistle to the Romans* (Grand Rapids, MI: Eerdmans, 1959, 1965), p. 59.

[9] See, for example, Philip Edgcumbe Hughes, *A Commentary on the Epistle to the Hebrews* (Grand Rapids, MI: Eerdmans, 1977), pp. 206-222, esp. p. 221; F. F. Bruce, *The Epistle to the Hebrews* (Grand Rapids, MI: Eerdmans, 1964), pp. 118-124; John Piper, "When Is Saving Repentance Impossible? Hebrews 6:4-8." See https://www.desiringgod.org/messages/when-is-saving-repentance-impossible; Steven J. Cole, "When Repentance Becomes Impossible (Hebrews 6:4-8)." See https://bible.org/seriespage/lesson-17-when-repentance-becomes-impossible-hebrews-64-8.

and loses everlasting life.[10] Still others interpret this section to mean that eternal salvation can be lost through apostasy.[11] All three of these views see repentance as a condition for everlasting life.

Yet Hebrews 6:4-8 is not talking about the repentance of *unbelievers* and it is not talking about a merely hypothetical situation. The author is discussing what happens when born again people apostatize. The point is that if the Jewish believing readers went so far as to turn their backs on Christ and to turn again to animal sacrifices as their basis for forgiveness, they would in effect be crucifying Jesus again and putting him to open shame. If they did that, then they would reap severe temporal judgment. The illustration of Hebrews 6:7-8 proves the point. If the ground yields a good crop, blessings result. If the ground yields thorns and thistles, curses result. The worthless overgrowth will be burned off, but, of course, the ground, representing the believer, remains.

What the believer loses if he apostatizes is temporal well-being, his physical life (premature death), and eternal rewards.[12]

James 5:19-20

"Brethren, if anyone among you wanders from the truth, and someone turns him back, let him know that he who turns a sinner from the error of his way will save a soul from death and cover a multitude of sins."

---

[10] See, for example, Donald Guthrie, *Hebrews* (Grand Rapids, MI: Eerdmans, 1983), p. 145; Albert Barnes, *Barnes' Notes on the New Testament* (Grand Rapids, MI: Kregel, 1832, 1834, 1962), p. 1267; Charles C. Ryrie, *The Ryrie Study Bible* (Chicago, IL: Moody Press, 1976, 1978), p. 1843, note on Hebrews 6:4-6.

[11] See, for example, Daniel D. Corner, *The Believer's Conditional Security: Eternal Security Refuted* (Washington, PA: Evangelical Outreach, 2000), pp. 308-18 (he suggests that salvation once lost can be regained as long as one has not committed what he calls "the eternal sin," pp. 319-20); *Systematic Theology: A Pentecostal Perspective*, edited by Stanley M. Horton (Springfield, MO: Logion Press, 1994), pp. 282-83, 370; kangaroodort (pen name), "Perseverance of the Saints, Part 5: Hebrews 6:4-9," at https://bible.org/seriespage/lesson-17-when-repentance-becomes-impossible-hebrews-64-8 (Arminian Perspectives website).

[12] This view is held by Zane Hodges, s.v., "Hebrews," in *The Bible Knowledge Commentary*, New Testament Edition (NP: Victor Books, 1983), pp. 794-96; R. T. Kendall, *Once Saved, Always Saved* (Chicago, IL: Moody Press, 1983), pp. 175-79; Charles Stanley, *Eternal Security* (Nashville, TN: Thomas Nelson Publishers, 1990), pp. 162-69.

Though the words *repent* and *repentance* are not found here, the concept of repentance ("he who turns a sinner from the error of his way") is in view.

The words "anyone among you" refer to anyone among the "brethren," that is, to believers. Only believers can wander from the truth. Unbelievers are not in the truth in the first place.

James's point is that if a fellow believer "turns him back," then he will "save a soul [= life] from death and cover a multitude of sins." The issue is not salvation from eternal condemnation, though that is a common interpretation.[13] It is the salvation of a fellow believer from the deadly temporal consequences of his straying away from the truth.

Conclusion

None of these texts come close to saying that the one who repents has everlasting life. These texts all deal with repentance as a condition for escaping temporal judgment and for gaining (or regaining) God's blessings in this life.

---

[13] See, for example, George M. Stulac, *James* (Downers Grove, IL: IVP Academic, 1993), p. 188; Peter Davids, *The Epistle of James* (Grand Rapids, MI: Eerdmans, 1982), pp. 199-201; D. Edmond Hiebert, *The Epistle of James* (Chicago, IL: Moody Press, 1979), pp. 334-35.

CHAPTER 16

Repentance and the Gospel of John

The Words *Repent* and *Repentance* Are Not Found in John

JOHN'S GOSPEL HAS OFTEN been called *The Gospel of Belief*, for the word *believe* occurs 100 times in John's Gospel. John repeatedly quotes the Lord Jesus as saying that whoever believes in Him has everlasting life and will never hunger, will never thirst, will never perish, will never die (John 3:16; 5:24; 6:35, 47; 11:25-26; 20:31).

The polar opposite of the number of uses of *believe* in John's Gospel is the number of uses of *repent* and *repentance*. Those words do not occur at all in John's Gospel.

John does use the verb *repent* a dozen times in the Book of Revelation. He was a disciple of John the Baptist before he was a disciple of Jesus (see John 1:35-40). So John was well aware of the preaching of repentance. But he does not once mention repentance in his Gospel. Not once.

The Concept of Repentance Is Not Found in John

Recognizing the significance of the absence of repentance in John's Gospel, some have suggested that while the words are not present, *the concept of repentance* is present.[1]

---

[1] See David A. Croteau, "Repentance Found? The Concept of Repentance in the Fourth Gospel," *The Master's Seminary Journal* (Spring 2013): 108-109; Wayne Grudem, *"Free Grace" Theology: 5 Ways It Diminishes the Gospel* (Wheaton, IL: Crossway, 2016), p. 52; John F. MacArthur, Jr., "Repentance in the Gospel of John." See https://www.gty.org/library/articles/A238/repentance-in-the-gospel-of-john.

However, when we look at what they call *the concept of repentance* in John, it is not actually the concept of repentance.[2] Wayne Grudem, for example, suggests that the concept of repentance is present 1) in the promise that the Holy Spirit will convict the world of sin, righteousness, and judgment (John 16:8), 2) in Jesus telling the woman at the well, "Go, call your husband, and come here" (John 4:16), and 3) in calls to faith in John's Gospel, which he thinks imply calls to repentance (e.g., John 1:11-12; 3:16; 4:14; 6:35, 37, 44, 53-56; 7:37).[3] None of those are calls to turn from one's sins.[4]

John MacArthur has a bigger list. He says,

> [Jesus] teaches that all true believers love the light (3:19), come to the light (3:20-21), obey the Son (3:36), practice the truth (3:21), worship in spirit and truth (4:23-24), honor God (5:22-24), do good deeds (5:29), eat Jesus' flesh and drink His blood (6:48-66), love God (8:42, cf. 1 John 2:15), follow Jesus (10:26-28), and keep Jesus' commandments (14:15).[5]

None of those references deal with turning from sins either.[6]

The call to repentance is a call to turn from one's sins. There is no such call in the Fourth Gospel.[7]

---

[2] Charlie Bing, "Is Repentance in John's Gospel?" See http://www.gracelife.org/resources/gracenotes/?id=83.
[3] Grudem, *5 Ways*, p. 52.
[4] An article by me entitled, "Is the Concept of Repentance Found in John's Gospel, and If So, What Difference Does It Make?" is projected to be published in *Journal of the Grace Evangelical Society* soon.
[5] MacArthur, "Repentance in John."
[6] For more discussion see Wilkin, "Is the Concept of Repentance Found in John's Gospel?"
[7] The closest to the concept in John's Gospel are "Go and sin no more" (John 8:11) and "Sin no more, lest a worse thing come upon you" (John 5:14). Both of those refer to specific sins that lead to serious temporal judgment: adultery and stoning in the first case and an unnamed sin and paralysis in the second case. Neither is a call to turn from all of one's sins. In addition, neither of those contexts is evangelistic. This is the strongest of Croteau's suggested references to the concept of repentance in John. But even it falls short.

The Absence of Repentance in John's Gospel Is a Powerful Argument about Silence

One final way to lessen the impact of the absence of repentance in John's Gospel is to say that this is an argument from silence, and arguments from silence prove nothing.

Actually, it is *an argument about silence*. Let's say that a famous historian wrote a book entitled, *The Greatest Generals of World War Two*. Now imagine that this historian did not mention General George Patton at all in his book. It would be certain that the historian did not consider General Patton one of the greatest generals of WW2.

In the same way, since John's purpose is evangelistic (John 20:31), and since he does not mention repentance, the conclusion is unmistakable (unless one reads his own theology into John's Gospel) that John teaches that repentance is not a condition of everlasting life.

John repeatedly indicates that the one and only condition for an individual Jew (or Gentile) to be born again is faith in Jesus Christ (e.g., John 3:16; 5:24; 6:35, 37, 39, 47; 11:25-27). Individual repentance is not required for the new birth. However, national repentance (which includes the individual repentance of all adults in the nation) is required for the kingdom to come for Israel. At the time of the Second Coming, Israel will be a believing nation in fellowship with God.

Scripture Consistently Teaches the Faith-Alone Message

When I first was confronted with the idea that repentance is not a condition of everlasting life, I doubted it could be true because of the ten passages which I discuss in Chapters 5-14. None of those ten passages were from John's Gospel. I was aware of the argument that John's Gospel is evangelistic and does not mention repentance. But at the time I considered repentance to be a synonym for faith, and so I saw the concept in John's Gospel. Besides, since Scripture can't contradict Scripture, if ten passages outside John teach that repentance is a condition of everlasting life, then John's Gospel cannot deny that is true.

Over the course of seven years I studied those ten passages. One by one I became convinced that those passages were not talking about what one must do to be saved from eternal condemnation. Once my objection concerning those ten passages vanished, I changed my view of repentance. That is, I became convinced that repentance is not a condition of everlasting life.

When that happened, the idea that the concept of repentance is in John's Gospel ceased to be a consideration. I had come to believe that repentance is turning from sins and that it is not a synonym for faith. Nowhere else does the New Testament teach that repentance is a condition of everlasting life. John's Gospel agrees that the sole condition of eternal salvation is faith in the Lord Jesus Christ.

The reason why some see the concept of repentance in John's Gospel is that they think it must be there if John's Gospel is evangelistic and if other Scriptures teach that repentance is a condition for everlasting life. But if other Scriptures don't teach that, then there is no reason to try to find something in John's Gospel that isn't there.

The faith-alone message is found throughout the New Testament (see Appendix 5). However, no book in the New Testament emphasizes that message more than John's Gospel. Merrill Tenney famously subtitled his study of John's Gospel as *The Gospel of Belief*.[8] There are 99 uses of the verb believe (*pisteuō*) in John's Gospel.

Salvation by faith alone means just that. It does not mean salvation by faith plus works, by faith plus baptism, by faith plus confession, by faith plus repentance, by faith plus self-denial, by faith plus cross bearing, by faith plus submission, by faith plus commitment, or by faith plus anything else at all.[9]

---

[8] Merrill C. Tenney, *John: The Gospel of Belief: An Analytical Study of the Text* (Grand Rapids, MI: Eerdmans, 1948, 1976).
[9] W. O. Vaught, Jr., Bill Clinton's pastor in the seventies at Immanuel Baptist Church in Little Rock, wrote a book entitled *Believe, Plus Nothing* (N.p.: n.p., 1983). After saying that "The unsaved man can repent of only one sin, and that is the sin of unbelief," he adds, "The only thing a sinner can do to be saved is to believe in Christ, change his mind about Christ. Therefore, sin is not the issue in salvation; Christ is the issue" (p. 22).

CHAPTER 17

Preaching Repentance and Salvation

Preaching Salvation

I REALIZE THAT MOST of you reading these words are not preachers. You do not have a literal pulpit to preach in.

However, you do have your own pulpit. It may be your dining room table where you teach your children over meals. It may be your children's bedside, where you teach them as you tuck them in at night. It might be the Sunday school class you teach. Or your home Bible study. Or your sharing of your faith with your relatives, your coworkers, and your neighbors.

We all have platforms that give us an opportunity to talk with others about Christ.

When you have that opportunity, what do you say? I remember my first class on the doctrine of salvation with Dr. Charles Ryrie. He said, "You are driving home from seminary. There is a terrible accident. You get out of your car and the police are asking for a minister. You confess you are a minister in training. The officer says you will do. He tells you the person is dying and has less than a minute to live. Write down in 25 words or less what you would tell that dying man he must do to be saved."

I wrote down something like this: *Jesus Christ died on the cross for your sins. If you believe in Him, He will give you everlasting life which can never be lost.*

You find that message in John 3:16; 5:24; 6:35, 47; 11:25-27; Acts 16:30-31; Ephesians 2:8-9; Revelation 22:17, and a host of other passages.

The condition is faith in Christ. The consequence is everlasting life which can never be lost. The condition is not good works, turning from sins, promising to serve God, perseverance in faith and works, or anything of the kind. Faith alone. Apart from works.

Preaching Repentance

Once again, how do you use your opportunities to talk to others about the subject of repentance?

In the course of everyday conversation, we can and should impress upon our children, extended family, friends, and co-workers the deadly consequences of living in the spiritual far country. To be away from God and from His teachings is very bad for you and for all those around you.

Typically, in my church ministry I preach about repentance when I come to it while teaching through a book. That happens a lot, since repentance is found all over the Bible.

I find it easy to preach repentance when the text talks about it. Of course, many people in church do not need to repent (see Appendix 3). Believers who are in fellowship with God need simply to confess their sins (1 John 1:9), not repent. Believers only need to repent when they have departed from fellowship with God (Luke 15:11-24).

But believers need teaching about repentance.

I grew up in Southern California in an area where there were rattlesnakes. I remember some guides showing us rattlesnakes in a wilderness area a few miles from my house and telling us how to avoid being bitten. They also told what to do if we were bitten. They did not wait until someone was already bitten to give the instruction. They gave the training in advance.

In the same way, Christians who are walking in fellowship with God need training about the dangers of sin and how to avoid it. They also need instruction on what to do if they are bitten and injected with sin's poison. We should not wait until our child or friend has become an immoral drug addict before we tell him about sin's deadly consequences and the importance of repentance if we fall. It is part of Christian maturity to know that rebelling against the Lord is very bad for you.

Believers need to repent if they depart from the Lord and go into the spiritual far country (Luke 15:11-24). The believer who strays needs to repent in order to escape ongoing temporal judgment and in order to regain the blessings of God in his life. And he needs to repent so that he can begin once again blessing those around him. It is much more fulfilling to be a blessing to our loved ones than a curse.

The regular proclamation of repentance in church helps renew the minds of believers and thereby transform their lives (Rom 12:1-2; 2 Cor 3:18). Believers with "the mind of Christ" (1 Cor 2:16) realize that the spiritual far country offers famine, hunger, pain, and suffering (Luke 15:11-19). Fellowship with God is better than anything this world has to offer (Luke 15:20-32). Walking in the light produces a life of joy and contentment. Spiritually-minded believers are also ready to rescue believers who have strayed (Jas 5:19-20) and to help other believers who are currently in fellowship with God to avoid the terrible consequences of walking in the darkness.

Keeping the Two Messages Distinct

It is important that we keep the two messages separate. They involve different conditions and different consequences.

If you are out of fellowship with God and want to escape God's temporal judgment and to regain His blessings, then the condition is turning from your sins and walking in the light of God's Word (Luke 15:11-32; Rom 12:1-2; 2 Cor 3:18).

If you want to escape eternal condemnation and to receive everlasting life, then the condition is believing in the Lord Jesus Christ (John 3:16). Of course, once you've believed in Him, you have everlasting life which can never be lost (John 11:26).

Two different conditions and two different consequences.

Keep those messages distinct whenever you talk with friends, family, and neighbors. Otherwise, you will confuse people. If they think that in order to be born again, they must believe in Jesus *and turn from their sins,* then they do not believe the message of John 3:16. They think that faith in Christ is necessary, but not enough. They must add reformation of their life. We can confuse people about what they must do to have everlasting life if we tell them that they must do more than believe in Jesus to have everlasting life.[1] While God can override false teaching, we

---

[1] In an online article entitled, "How to Preach Repentance," Mark Spence of Living Waters Ministry mixes up the two messages. He says, "repentance is required in order to have a relationship with God and go to Heaven." He adds, "Jesus warned, 'Unless you repent, you

are hindering people from coming to faith in Christ if we teach that the new birth requires both repentance and faith.

The opposite is also true. We dare not give the impression that simply by believing in Jesus we will have fullness of life and the blessings of God. The new birth does not guarantee God's blessings in this life. In order to have His blessings, we must walk in the light of God's Word. We must avoid yielding to sin in our experience.

---

will perish' (Luke 13:3). Repentance is more than feeling sorry for your sin. Of course, you should feel sorry for your sins; you have done wrong. The question is, are you willing to turn from your sins and turn toward God, to place your faith in Christ and surrender your life to Him today?" See https://www.livingwaters.com/how-to-preach-repentance/. See also Steven Lawson, "Should I Always Call for Repentance and Faith," https://www.thegospelcoalition.org/article/preachers-toolkit-should-i-always-call-for-repentance-faith/.

CHAPTER 18

Conclusion: Repentance Is a Vital Biblical Doctrine

CHURCH HISTORY GOT THE doctrine of repentance wrong soon after the Apostles left the scene. Repentance was quickly seen as the way in which a person who committed a major sin could get his salvation back. After a short time in which only one opportunity for getting one's salvation back was allowed, the early church allowed for multiple times to repent and regain salvation. But they set up rules to regulate repentance. A priest had to hear the confession and then decide what acts of repentance, called acts of penance, would be required in order to get one's salvation back.

The doctrine of repentance was so bad at the time of the Reformation that people could buy indulgences to be able to plan out their sin and get forgiveness in advance, for a price. Luther rejected such a man-made doctrine. He and John Calvin taught that everlasting life was gained by faith alone, apart from works.

Shortly after Luther and Calvin, their followers established repentance as a condition for the new birth. One had to turn from sins and believe in Christ in order to be born again.

Today most people in Christendom believe that repentance is either required to be born again and/or in order to regain one's salvation after committing a major sin.

The Old Testament has a robust teaching on repentance. Much of the preaching of repentance in the Old Testament is directed toward national Israel. The people had to corporately repent for deliverance to come. This was especially evident in the Book of Judges.

There was also a call in the Old Testament for individual Jews to turn from their sins in order to escape calamity and premature death (e.g., Ezekiel 18).

The Old Testament does not say much about regeneration or justification. But it does teach justification by faith alone (e.g., Gen 15:6). It does not teach justification or regeneration by repentance.

The New Testament, unlike the Old Testament, emphasizes individual repentance. There is not much on national repentance outside of the Synoptic Gospels in which the Lord Jesus and John the Baptist repeatedly called for national repentance.[1]

While there are ten New Testament passages which seem to teach that repentance is a condition for everlasting life, it is evident upon careful analysis that none of them do. The consistent teaching of the New Testament, as highlighted by the Lord Jesus' evangelistic preaching in John's Gospel, is that regeneration is by faith alone, apart from works.

There are many wonderful cures for diseases today. Some are vaccines that keep you from getting the disease in the first place. I'm thinking here of the annual flu shots, the polio vaccine, vaccines for measles, etc.

There are also medicines that can be given to stop a disease already in progress. Antivenom stops the ongoing effects of venom. Statin drugs drop one's cholesterol count and reduce the risk of heart attack and stroke.

Repentance is the latter sort of medicine. It is the remedy for one who has fallen away from the Lord and who is experiencing temporal judgment. By turning from his sins, he can stop the progress of his spiritual disease. Damage has already been done. But further damage can be avoided if a person repents.

However, repentance *preaching* is a preventative medicine too. If believers who are walking in fellowship with God regularly hear of the terrible wages of sin, they will be far less likely to stray.

This medicine is for believers and unbelievers alike. That is why 12-step programs are often effective. If people turn from their wicked ways, then God will lessen or even cease the deadly consequences which they had been experiencing.

---

[1] There are re-offers of the kingdom in Acts, and some of these include calls for national repentance (e.g., Acts 3:19). And 2 Peter 3:9 looks at the need for enough worldwide repentance to continue in order for the Tribulation and its billions of deaths to be postponed.

(I should mention, however, that if a person attends a 12-step program for alcoholism, for example, he has not necessarily repented even if he stops drinking. While many in 12-step programs turn from all their sins, some only turn from drunkenness. A sober person can be immoral, a liar, a cheat, and in rebellion against God.

Repentance is a decision to turn from all one's sins, plural. It is not merely a turning from one issue in life.)

The believer who is walking with Christ does not need to repent. After all, he is walking with Christ. He is not intentionally rebelling against the Lord.

When the spiritually healthy believer recognizes he has sinned, he merely confesses his sin, and he can continue to walk in fellowship with God (1 John 1:7-9). Confession, not repentance, is his need.

Of course, there is inherent in confession a desire to not repeat committing the sin in question. But the Bible never calls confession *repentance*. The two are distinct. Repentance is for willful departure from the Lord (Luke 15:11-24).

Repentance is not a cure for eternal condemnation. An unbeliever who turns from his sins remains spiritually dead. He has *taken a step toward God*, as I often heard Dr. Criswell say at his altar calls. But the one who has taken a step toward God has not been born again unless and until he has believed in Jesus for everlasting life.

Now, repentance can lead to a person coming to faith in Christ. He might start attending church and hearing God's Word taught. Through hearing the good news of Jesus Christ, he can come to faith and be born again. While repentance is not required to come to faith in Christ, it certainly can be an impetus to faith in Him.

Sadly, history repeats itself. Many well-intentioned people continue to radically confuse the evangelistic message by means of faulty teaching on repentance. Many people think that repentance is a condition, or the condition, of everlasting life. They believe and teach that faith in Christ is ineffective unless it is joined with repentance.

Pastors and teachers advocating repentance as a condition for everlasting life mean well. They want people to be born again. And they want people to live for Christ and to have happy lives. So, they figure that repentance is a way to make those things happen.

But telling a person he must repent to be born again is like telling a person who has colon cancer that if he gives up smoking, he will be healed. Stopping smoking won't cure cancer. In order to get over cancer, you need to get rid of the malignancy within you, either by surgery, radiation, chemo, or a combination of all three. And, unlike faith in Christ, the success rate is not 100%.

If a person believes in the Lord Jesus Christ for everlasting life, he will always gain everlasting life even if he has major areas of sin in his life.[2]

Now stopping smoking is a great thing to do no matter what kind of cancer you have. It may keep you from getting cancer again if you go into remission. But it is not a cure for cancer.

But in the case of spiritual birth, once you gain everlasting life, you can never lose it. There is no spiritual un-birth. Everlasting life is everlasting life. Once a person believes in Christ for everlasting life, he is secure forever.

But the new believer can fail to grow. If a new believer does not plug into a solid Bible-teaching church and begin the process of discipleship, then he will experience the judgment of God concerning his ungodly lifestyle and his failure to grow in his faith.

The Lord never said that repentance is a condition for everlasting life. He repeatedly said that *whoever believes in Him has everlasting life.* Belief. Not repentance.

Of course, the Lord did preach repentance. But not for everlasting life.

So we should preach repentance too. But not for everlasting life.

You wouldn't tell an unbeliever that if he turns from his sinful ways, starts going to church, praying, and studying the Bible, then God guarantees him everlasting life. But you would encourage an unbeliever to do all those things. They are for his own good. And those things can result in his coming to faith in Christ.

---

[2] At the very moment of faith, a person begins the Christian life with a clean slate (Acts 10:43). The new believer does not need to repent. He needs to grow. No matter how many sinful ways he has, growth occurs by getting into Christian instruction (Heb 10:23-25). However, it is possible that shortly after the new birth, a believer might stumble so badly that repentance is called for. Peter does tell a new believer, Simon Magus, "Repent therefore of this your wickedness, and pray God if perhaps the thought of your heart may be forgiven you" (Acts 8:22-23). Simon's sin was not limited to trying to buy the ability to convey the Holy Spirit by the laying on of hands. His whole attitude was wrong. He was evidently still craving the acclaim and attention that came when people called him "the great power of God" (Acts 8:10).

Repentance is powerful. Nineveh was spared when it repented at the preaching of Jonah. Our country has been spared thus far because enough people have repented that the level of wickedness does not demand our destruction.

Use the right medicine for the right illness. That is a good practice for medical doctors. And it is a good practice for spiritual doctors.

APPENDIX 1

Why So Many Think Repentance Is a Condition of Everlasting Life

IF YOU LISTEN TO just about any pastor preaching about what one must do to have everlasting life they'll say that repentance and faith are required. This is true in Southern Baptist circles. American Baptist. GARBC. Independent Baptist. Hardshell Baptist. Church of Christ. Assembly of God. Bible churches. Community churches. Foursquare. Evangelical Free churches. Methodist churches. And so forth.

Most commentaries on the books of the New Testament identify faith and repentance as required to be born again.

This thinking is very ingrained in Evangelicalism today. But why? I suggest that there are three main reasons for this belief.

Reason #1: It Seems Reasonable That People Must Repent to Be Born Again

If people could be born again simply by faith in Christ, apart from repentance, then at least some unrepentant people would be saved. It seems unreasonable that unrepentant people can be saved. Surely, in order to be saved by faith in Christ, one must first be repentant.

It is possible, in this way of thinking, to see faith in Christ as the main condition of the new birth and repentance as a necessary precursor to faith. But regardless of how it is explained, most people in Evangelicalism today think that it is obvious that repentance must be joined with faith in Christ in order for a person to be born again.

Reason #2: Tradition Going Back to the Early Church Teaches Repentance for Eternal Salvation

A second reason, one that follows on the heels of the first, is that this view is widely held today, and it has been widely held since the second century. How can so many people be so wrong?

Tradition is a powerful force. If many different Evangelical traditions all teach that repentance is a condition for everlasting life, then it seems logical that it must be true. Surely the majority could not be wrong, especially the majority over two millennia.

Reason #3: Passages That Seem to Condition Salvation on Repentance

As we saw in Chapters 5-14, there are ten passages which appear to be slam-dunk proofs that repentance is a condition of everlasting life. The Lord and His apostles said the following about repentance and salvation:

1. "Repent, for the kingdom of heaven is at hand" (Matt 3:2; 4:17).
2. "Repent and believe the gospel" (Mark 1:15).
3. "Unless you repent you will all likewise perish" (Luke 13:3, 5).
4. "If one goes to them from the dead, they will repent" (Luke 16:30).
5. "Repentance and forgiveness shall be preached" (Luke 24:47).
6. "Repent and you shall receive the gift of the Holy Spirit" (Acts 2:38).
7. "God has granted the Gentiles repentance to life" (Acts 11:18).
8. "Godly sorrow produces repentance leading to salvation" (2 Cor 7:10).
9. "Turning to God from idols" (1 Thess 1:9).
10. "God wishes none to perish, but for all to come to repentance" (2 Pet 3:9).

People look at verses such as those and see confirmation of what tradition teaches and of what seems completely reasonable. That is, people must repent in order to be born again.

And there are a few other passages which, though less compelling, also seem to support repentance as a condition for everlasting life:
1. "I did not come to call the righteous, but sinners, to repentance" (Matt 9:13; Mark 2:17; Luke 5:32).
2. "So they went out and preached that people should repent" (Mark 6:12).
3. "There will be more joy in heaven over one sinner who repents than over ninety-nine just persons who need no repentance" (Luke 15:7).
4. "Repent therefore and be converted, that your sins may be blotted out, so that the time of refreshing may come from the presence of the Lord" (Acts 3:19).
5. "I...taught you publicly and from house to house, testifying to Jews, and also to Greeks, repentance toward God and faith toward our Lord Jesus Christ" (Acts 20:20-21).
6. "Therefore, King Agrippa, I was not disobedient to the heavenly vision, but declared first to those in Damascus and in Jerusalem, and throughout all the region of Judea, and then to the Gentiles, that they should repent, turn to God, and do works befitting repentance" (Acts 26:19-20).
7. "A servant of the Lord must...be...able to teach, patient, in humility correcting those who are in opposition, if perhaps God will grant them repentance, so that they may know the truth, and that they may come to their senses and escape the snare of the devil, having been taken captive by him to do his will" (2 Tim 2:24-26).

But None of Those Reasons Are Convincing

We should never judge truth based on whether it seems reasonable to us. For the vast majority of people in the world today, the death penalty is unreasonable and abortion, even infanticide, is reasonable. Yet the Bible supports the former but not the latter. Who is right: God or "reason"?

Judging truth on poll numbers is a terrible idea as well. It really does not matter what percentage of people who call themselves Christians believe that one must repent in order to be born again. What matters is what God says. The majority is often wrong.

The third reason has the most merit because it is based on Scripture. However, it is not compelling for the following reasons:

- With the exception of Luke 16:30, which are the words of an unregenerate man who is being tormented in Hades, and possibly Acts 11:18, which are the words of Jewish believers, none of those passages is even dealing with the new birth. They all deal with *salvation from temporal judgment.*
- Whatever those passages mean cannot contradict the clear teaching we find in over 100 verses in the New Testament (see Appendix 5). There are over a hundred faith-alone verses. John 3:16, for example, says "whoever believes in Him…has everlasting life." There is no mention of repentance in John 3:16, or in all of John's Gospel. Nor is repentance mentioned in Paul's defense of his gospel in Galatians.
- If regeneration is by faith alone, and it is, then it is not by faith plus repentance. As obvious as that is, I've heard many preachers say, "Salvation is by faith alone, so if you simply repent of your sins and believe in Jesus you will be saved." Regeneration is not by faith alone if repentance is a co-condition.
- Repentance is a work, something other than believing (Matt 12:41; Jonah 3:10, "when God saw *their works, that they turned from their evil ways…*"). And yet salvation is "not of works, lest anyone should boast" (Eph 2:9; John 6:28-29).
- The practical problem with this view is that if one must turn from his sins to be born again, then he must stop sinning to be born again. So, people water this down in the following ways:
    1. You need only turn from *the particular sin or sins of which God is convicting you* (premarital sex, homosexuality, drunkenness, etc.).
    2. You need only turn *from the sin(s) which God leads me to tell you* that you need to turn from.
    3. You only need *to be willing to turn from all your sins.* If this willingness is genuine, then as you grow as a Christian you will turn from your sins.
    4. You need *to have regret over your sins and a desire to live differently.* You do not actually need to turn from your sins. But you must be sorry and you must want to live for God.

- Since I do not have chapters explaining the seven additional passages I have mentioned above, I will briefly discuss each here:
  1. Matthew 9:13 and parallels have to do with Jesus' ministry of calling the nation to repentance so that the kingdom might come. See Chapter 5 on Matt 3:2 and Matt 4:17 for more details.
  2. That the Lord sent out the Twelve to preach repentance (and cast out demons and heal people, Mark 6:12-13) was part of His calling the nation to repentance. See Chapter 5.
  3. The Lord is speaking of the repentance *of believers* in Luke 15:7. There is more joy in heaven over one backslider who repents than over ninety-nine righteous believers "who need no repentance." None of the three parables of Luke 15 are a salvific passage.[1]
  4. The Apostles repeated the Lord's offers of the kingdom to Israel (Acts 3:19). The time of refreshing is the kingdom. The issue here was the kingdom coming. See Chapter 5.
  5. Paul preached both repentance toward God and faith in the Lord Jesus Christ (Acts 20:21). Those were two different aspects of his ministry. The latter was his evangelistic call as Acts 13:39 and Acts 16:31 show.

---

[1] Many commentators think that the words "ninety-nine just persons who need no repentance" are intended to be understood in an ironic (or sarcastic) sense. Therefore, they suggest that the Lord was actually referring to the scribes and Pharisees who *wrongly thought they were righteous and who wrongly thought that they did not need to repent, but who actually were not righteous and who did need to repent.* W. R. F. Browning says that Luke 15:7 is a rebuke against "The self-righteous [who] have not begun to see the need for repentance" (*St. Luke* [Norwich, Great Britain: SCM Press Ltd, 1960, 1965, 1972], p. 130). Darrell Bock agrees (*A Theology of Luke and Acts* [Grand Rapids, MI: Zondervan, 2012], pp. 263-64). Pate, however, is undecided: "It is a matter of debate as to whether or not Jesus' mention of ninety-nine who need not repent is ironic. If so, it would have been a veiled criticism of the Pharisees' and scribes' perception of themselves as righteous. If not, it would be a matter-of-fact comment" (C. Marvin Pate, *Luke* [Chicago, IL: Moody Press, 1995], pp. 302-303). There is nothing in the context to suggest that this is an ironic statement. The sheep that was lost was originally with the other ninety-nine. The coin that was lost was originally with the other nine. The son who was lost was originally with his Father and older brother. This all suggests that Luke 15:7 is "a matter-of-fact comment." Leon Morris evidently understands it in a straightforward way since he writes concerning Luke 15:7 that "He rejoices over the returning penitent more than *over many safely in the fold*" (*Luke*, Revised Edition [Grand Rapids, MI: Eerdmans, 1974, 1988], p. 261, emphasis added).

The former was both pre-evangelistic (Acts 17:30) and discipleship (see Chapter 12, 2 Cor 7:10).

6. Paul clearly did preach repentance, turning to God, and doing works that befit repentance (Acts 26:20). But he never said that repentance is a condition of everlasting life.

7. "Those in opposition" refers to believers who were once in fellowship with God but who were taken captive by the devil (2 Tim 2:24-26). Elders need to be able to correct such people "so that they may know the truth, and that they may come to their senses." The issue here is not salvific.

Conclusion

Why are so many so wrong about repentance and salvation? Why has this error continued among the majority of Christendom for nearly two thousand years? This is because of reason, tradition, and a misinterpretation of ten to twenty passages. But we follow Scripture, not reason and not tradition.

The Lord did not mention repentance in John 3:14-18. Or John 4:7-26. Or John 5:24. Or John 6:35, 37, 39, 47. Or John 11:25-27. In fact, the words *repent* and *repentance* do not occur at all in John's Gospel, which has an evangelistic purpose (John 20:30-31). We know from John's Gospel and Galatians (where repentance also is not found) that repentance isn't a condition of the new birth. A careful study of the passages supposedly teaching that repentance is a condition of the new birth shows that not one of them teaches that.

It is time that we return to Jesus' faith-alone message. The promise of life is for whoever believes in Him. It really is that simple. Keep it simple, saint.

APPENDIX 2

Why the Change-of-Mind View of Repentance Is Inaccurate

As I progressed in my classes at Dallas Theological Seminary, I was puzzled by the role of repentance in salvation from eternal condemnation. This led me to write my doctoral dissertation on "The Role of Repentance in Salvation in the New Testament."

Here was what puzzled me. I knew that salvation from condemnation is by faith alone. The word *alone* means *by itself, without addition*. So salvation could not be by faith plus repentance.

Yet I felt there were about ten passages in the New Testament which clearly taught that repentance is a condition for everlasting life.

I discovered that the founder of DTS, Dr. Lewis Sperry Chafer, as well as one of my professors, Dr. Charles Ryrie, held to something called *the change-of-mind view of repentance*. In this understanding, repentance refers to a change of mind about self and Christ. A person must come to see that he cannot save himself, and he must come to see Christ as the One who gives him everlasting life as a free gift. In this understanding, repentance is a synonym for faith.

I argued for that position in my dissertation. People who still hold to the change-of-mind view like my dissertation. However, about a dozen years after I handed in the final draft of my dissertation, I changed my mind about repentance. I came to believe that repentance is always changing your mind *about your sins*. It is always a decision to turn from one's sinful ways to the Lord. In addition, I came to see that repentance is never a condition for everlasting life.

There are several terrific things I like about the change-of-mind-about-Christ view. It says that turning from sins is not a condition of everlasting life. It goes further and says that even a desire to turn from one's sins or a desire for a new way of life is not required. Nor is remorse over one's sins required. According to this understanding, faith in Christ (= repentance) is all that is required. However, I have come to reject my former position for four reasons.

Reason #1: The Words *Metanoia* and *Metanoeō* Are Not Synonyms for Faith

First, the simplest way to prove that these words are not synonymous is to find places in the New Testament which use both words in the same verse. Repentance and faith or believe (*pistis* or *pisteuō*) occur in the same verse only four times in the New Testament (Mark 1:15; Acts 19:4; 20:21; Heb 6:1). In each of those texts, believing and repentance are two separate things.

Second, the other way is to determine what each word's field of meaning is. The *pistis/pisteuō* word group primarily means *to be persuaded, to be convinced* (e.g., Matt 9:28; John 8:24; 11:25-27; 20:31; Acts 8:12; 9:26; Rom 6:8; 1 Thess 4:14; Heb 11:6; 1 John 5:1).[1] In a small number of texts it means to entrust or to commit (e.g., John 2:24; 1 Cor 9:17; Gal 2:7; 1 Thess 2:4; 1 Tim 1:11; Titus 1:3).[2] It never once means *to turn from sins, to turn from wicked ways*.

The *metanoia/metanoeō* word group mean *to repent, to turn from*.[3] It is certainly acceptable to stress the mental aspect of it and understand it as *to change one's mind about his sinful ways*.[4] But it never once means

---

[1] BDAG sees two main senses for *pisteuō*. First, "to consider something to be true and therefore worthy of one's trust, *believe*" (pp. 816-17). Second, "to entrust oneself to an entity in complete confidence, *believe (in), trust*" (pp. 817-18). It lists 89 verses under the first sense and 149 under the second sense.

[2] The third sense in BDAG for *pisteuō* is "entrust something to someone" (p. 818). BDAG lists eight verses under this usage. It only lists three verses in the final two senses, "be confident about" and "think/consider possible." None of the five senses is to change one's mind about Christ or anything else.

[3] The second meaning under *metanoeō* in BDAG, the only one it lists with New Testament examples, is "feel remorse, repent, be converted" (p. 64). It lists 35 verses which carry this sense. Not a single verse is understood to refer to a change of mind about Christ or anything else. Concerning the noun, *metanoia*, BDAG says it means "repentance, turning about, conversion" (p. 64). It lists 22 verses which carry this sense.

[4] However, while BDAG lists the meaning "change one's mind" first under *metanoeō*, because it is used that way in extra Biblical literature, it does not suggest a single verse in the New Testament in which it means that.

to be persuaded or *to be convinced*. And there is no context in which it refers specifically *to a change of mind about Christ*.

Many Biblical examples show that the words are not synonyms. In John 11:26, the Lord Jesus asks Martha, "Do you believe this?" He was referring to what He had just said about His being the resurrection and the life. He was asking her if she was convinced that what He had said is true. Her answer, as recorded in John 11:27, shows that she was convinced. He was not asking, "Do you change your mind about this?"

In Acts 8:22, Peter said to Simon Magus, "Repent therefore of this your wickedness." He was calling for him to turn from his wicked attitudes. He was not calling for him to change his mind about Christ.[5] Luke already told us in Acts 8:13, "Then Simon himself also believed." It was days later when Peter and John arrived, and Peter rebuked Simon.

The Lord said in Rev 2:21, "I gave her time to repent of her sexual immorality, and she did not repent." The issue here is a failure to turn from sins (or a failure to change her attitude about her sins), not a failure to change her mind about Christ.

Many other verses specify repentance *from sinful deeds* (see, for example, Revelation 2:22, "unless they repent of their deeds"; Revelation 9:20, "they did not repent of the works of their hands, that they should not worship demons, and idols…"; Revelation 9:21, "they did not repent of their murders or their sorceries or their sexual immorality or their thefts"; and Revelation 16:11, "they did not repent of their deeds"). The point is clear. Repentance in the New Testament is a call to turn from one's sins. It is not a call to faith in Christ.

In the New Testament, *metanoia* and *metanoeō* are not synonyms for faith as the change-of-mind view suggests. The change-of-mind-about-Christ view is not compatible with Scripture.[6]

---

[5] Since "this your wickedness" referred to Simon's attempt to buy the ability to convey the Holy Spirit by the laying on of hands, this might be understood as calling for a change of mind about God. However, that is not suggested by the context. That would be reading one's theology into the text. In any case, the call to repent of wickedness is not a call to faith in Christ since Simon already believed in Christ.

[6] The change-of-mind view sees repentance as a synonym for faith in Christ in many passages. But in the New Testament it is never a synonym for faith in Christ.

Reason #2: John's Gospel Is Evangelistic and Never Mentions Repentance

If repentance and faith are synonyms, then surely the Lord Jesus Christ used them interchangeably. But He did not. A study of the Synoptic Gospels, in which the terms are used by the Lord Jesus, shows that He does not use the words interchangeably. Further, the fact that John's Gospel is the only book in the Bible whose stated purpose is evangelistic (John 20:30-31), and yet it never once mentions repentance, is a show-stopper for the change-of-mind view.

It would have been easy for the Lord after John 3:16 and the words, "whoever believes in Him…has everlasting life," to use slightly different language in verse 18, "He who *repents* about Him is not condemned, but he who does not *repent* is condemned already, because he has not *repented* concerning the name of the only begotten Son of God." But the Lord uses *pisteuō* three times in verse 18, "believes…does not believe… has not believed."

I realize that this is just one encounter, Jesus evangelizing Nicodemus. But in the entire Gospel of John, the Lord does not once equate believing in Him with changing one's mind about Him.

Reason #3: Repentance Is Strikingly Absent in Paul

While there is no merit in the idea that Christian doctrine today is only found in Paul's epistles (or only in some of his epistles), it is nonetheless true that Paul is the leading author of the New Testament. He wrote thirteen (or fourteen) of the twenty-seven books. While Luke's writings are longer than Paul's, few Christians think that Luke's writings have more impact on the church today than Paul's.

Paul repeatedly wrote that the sole condition for everlasting life and justification is faith in Christ (e.g., Rom 3:22, 25, 26, 27, 28, 30; 4:3, 5, 11, 13, 20, 21, 24; 5:1; Gal 2:16; 3:5-14; Eph 2:8-9; 1 Tim 1:16).

James D. G. Dunn noted that the doctrine of repentance is "a category strikingly absent from Paul."[7]

If repentance means a change of mind about Christ, then we would expect to see that in Paul. Yet he only mentions repentance in three of

---

[7] James D. G. Dunn, "The Justice of God: A Renewed Perspective on Justification by Faith," *Journal of Theological Studies*, New Series, 43 (April 1992), p. 7.

Why the Change-of-Mind View Is Inaccurate   109

his thirteen epistles. There is no mention of repentance in 1 Corinthians, Galatians, Ephesians, Philippians, Colossians, 1 Thessalonians (though the concept is in 1:9), 2 Thessalonians, 1 Timothy, Titus, or Philemon.

There is one use in Romans, three uses in 2 Corinthians, and one in 2 Timothy. But none of those five are in contexts that explain what one must do to have everlasting life:

1. Romans 2:4, "not knowing that the goodness of God leads you to repentance." The moralist should be led to turn from his self-righteous attitudes and his legalistic moralism and turn to God to find the way of justification, which Paul proclaims in Rom 3:21-31 as faith in Christ. Paul does not mention repentance in the justification section of Romans. This is the one and only use. And Paul is not talking about a change of mind about Christ.
2. 2 Corinthians 7:9, "I rejoice...that your sorrow led to repentance." Paul was referring there to the *believers* in Corinth. They had tolerated a brother in the church living in sin with his own stepmother (1 Cor 5:1-13). The issue here was church discipline, not the new birth and not a change of mind about Christ.
3. 2 Corinthians 7:10, "For godly sorrow produces repentance leading to salvation, not to be regretted; but the sorrow of the world produces death...you sorrowed in a godly manner." Paul is still speaking of the repentance of the *believers* in Corinth. The *salvation* under discussion here is deliverance from God's temporal judgment. The issue is not the new birth. And the condition is not a change of mind about Christ.
4. 2 Corinthians 12:21, "lest, when I come again, my God will humble me among you, and I shall mourn for many who have sinned before and have not repented of the uncleanness, fornication, and lewdness which they have practiced." Paul is calling the *believers* in Corinth to turn from their sinful ways (uncleanness, fornication, lewdness). Clearly this is not a change of mind about Christ, and the issue is not the new birth.
5. 2 Timothy 2:25-26, "A servant of the Lord must...in humility correct those who are in opposition, if God perhaps will grant them repentance, so that they may know the truth, and that they may come to their senses and escape the snare of the devil,

having been taken captive to do his will." Paul is commanding Timothy to correct *believers* who are in opposition to his teaching so that they may repent. Timothy is teaching the truth. To reject his teaching is not to know the truth. These believers needed to come to their senses. When a believer opposes the clear teaching of God's Word, he is a pawn of the devil. The issue here is clearly not the new birth. Nor is a change of mind about Christ the point in 2 Timothy 2:25.

Reason #4: Regeneration Is Absent in Repentance Texts

A final fly in the ointment is the fact that only one of the texts cited says anything about everlasting life, the new birth, salvation from eternal condemnation, or anything like that. See Chapters 5-14. Here is a brief summary:

Passage	Consequence of Repenting
• Matthew 3:2 (and 4:17)	The kingdom will come now
• Mark 1:14-15	The kingdom will come now
• Luke 13: 3, 5	Avoid premature death
• Luke 16:19-31	See below
• Luke 24:47	Forgiveness of sins
• Acts 2:38	Reception of Spirit and forgiveness
• Acts 11:18	Fullness of physical life
• 2 Corinthians 7:10	Deliverance from temporal judgment
• 1 Thessalonians 1:9	Fullness of life
• 2 Peter 3:9	Avoid death and suffering worldwide

Luke 16:19-31 is the only one of the repentance texts (with the possible exception of Acts 11:18—see Chapter 11) which actually concerns regeneration.[8] However, the one claiming that repentance is the way to avoid torment in Sheol is the unregenerate rich man. Abraham, the believer, the one who is not in torment, insists that the only way to avoid eternal condemnation is by being persuaded and listening to (i.e., believing) Moses and the prophets. Luke 16:19-31

---

[8] Some think that the forgiveness of sins in Luke 24:47 is part of salvation and thus that it too might be an exception. See Chapter 9 for evidence that it is not dealing with salvation from eternal condemnation.

refutes the notion that repentance is a condition for escaping eternal condemnation.

Where is the verse which says, "He who repents has everlasting life"? Or, "He who comes to Me shall never hunger, and he who repents concerning Me shall never thirst"? Or, "Whoever lives and repents shall never die"? There is no such text.

Conclusion

The beauty of the change-of-mind-about-Christ view is that it appears to eliminate any problem passages related to repentance. Whenever repentance seems to be a condition of the new birth, then we can say that repentance there is a synonym for faith in Christ. Whenever repentance is thought not to be in a salvific context, then we can say that it refers to changing one's mind about one's sins.

In the first place, that does not eliminate scores of verses that are clearly talking about changing your mind *about your sinful ways,* not about Christ. If there are verses which indicate that repentance is a condition for everlasting life, then all of those texts become potential evangelistic texts. Nor does it eliminate the scores of verses that call for *turning from your sinful ways* (using the *-strephō* verbs). The change-of-mind-about-Christ view may satisfy some people. But it will not satisfy most people since it is easy to see in Scripture that repentance is turning from sins, not changing one's mind about Christ.

Dr. Ryrie was one of my favorite professors at DTS. He ordained me and preached my ordination sermon. He held to the change-of-mind-about-Christ view. Dick Seymour, who wrote a book defending the change-of-mind-about-Christ view,[9] is a friend and a strong proponent of the faith-alone message. I myself defended the change-of-mind-about-Christ view when I wrote my dissertation. So, I'm not suggesting that this understanding leads to false teaching about what one must do to be born again. What I'm saying is that it is not an accurate presentation of the Biblical teaching on repentance, and hence this view should be dropped.

I suppose I should have had second thoughts when I argued that most of the time in the New Testament, repentance is a change of mind

---

[9] Richard A. Seymour, *All About Repentance,* Second Edition (Lagrange, WY: Integrity Press, 1974, 2007).

about one's sinful ways. I argued that only in ten passages was repentance a change of mind about Christ. That allowed me to get around ten seeming problem texts. But it did not allow me to handle the context of those texts adequately.[10] I believe my explanations in Chapters 5-14 are much clearer than my explanations of those same ten texts in my dissertation.[11]

---

[10] Seymour has a chapter (Chapter 9) in the second edition of his book (see previous note) dealing with my view, which he calls the Rethinking Repentance Group (RRG for short). Unfortunately, he only gives two quotes from RRG advocates (pp. 135, 158), and he does not indicate who wrote them. Nor does he give bibliographic information. I think he is quoting me or maybe Zane Hodges. He goes through some of the ten passages which seem to teach that repentance is a condition of everlasting life (Luke 13: 3-5; 16:30; 24:47; Acts 2:38; 17:30; 2 Pet 3:9). His discussion, while certainly well written and persuasive for those who already hold the change-of-mind-about-Christ view, is not persuasive to those who do not hold to that view. See *All About Repentance*, Second Edition, pp. 127-62.

[11] I condensed my dissertation into six journal articles. You can see the way I handled those texts by going to the following links: "Repentance in the Gospels and Acts" (https://faithalone.org/journal/1990i/wilkin.html) and "Repentance in the Epistles and Revelation" (https://faithalone.org/journal/1990ii/wilkin.html).

APPENDIX 3

Righteous People Need No Repentance

REPENTANCE IS MISUNDERSTOOD AS a condition for salvation. But it is also misunderstood as a condition for ongoing fellowship with God. I realize that this comment will cause most readers to scratch their heads. For many people in Christianity, repentance is thought to be a vital every-day, if not moment-by-moment, experience.

About twenty years ago, a Christian friend told me that he thought a believer could go years or even decades in fellowship with God, without needing to repent. I was intrigued. My friend suggested the condition for ongoing fellowship is confession of our sins, not repenting of them. He felt that it was an error to equate confession with repentance or to say that confession includes repentance.

Upon doing further study, I concluded my friend was right. The Scriptures support the idea that repentance is not a condition for ongoing fellowship with God.

Evidence That Repentance Is Not for Believers in Fellowship with God

No Repentance Verses Deal with Believers in Fellowship

There are fifty-five uses of *repent* (*metanoeō*) and repentance (*metanoia*) in the New Testament. While a few of those uses are ambiguous, here is how those uses break down:

Calling unbelievers to turn from their sins (including national Israel). There are twenty-three uses (Matt 3:2, 8, 11; 4:17; 11:20, 21; 12:41; Mark 1:15; 6:12; Luke 10:13; 11:32;13:3, 5; Acts 3:19; 5:31; 13:24; 19:4;

17:30; Rom 2:4; Rev 9:20, 21; 16:9, 11). None of these verses promise everlasting life for those who repent, as we've seen in Chapters 4-16.

Calling believers who've strayed to turn from their sins. There are nineteen uses (Luke 15:7, twice, 10; Acts 2:38; 8:22; 2 Cor 7:9, 10; 12:21; 2 Tim 2:25; Heb 6:1, 6; Rev 2:5, twice, 16, 21, twice, 22; 3:3, 19). The issue in each case is for believers to return to fellowship with God (with 2 Tim 2:25 being a possible exception).

Verses calling both unbelievers and believers who are out of fellowship to turn from their sins. There are eight uses (Matt 9:13; Mark 1:4; 2:17; Luke 3:3, 8; 5:32; 24:27; 2 Pet 3:9). In none of these cases is repentance a condition for everlasting life, as seen in Chapters 4-16.

Verses dealing with interpersonal repentance. There are three uses (Luke 17:3, 4; Heb 12:17a).

Verses which are unclear whether they deal with believers or unbelievers. There are two uses (Acts 11:18; 20:21).

None of the verses calling for repentance are directed to believers who are currently in fellowship with God. That is telling.

The Righteous Do Not Need Repentance (Luke 15:7)

Whether the Lord was speaking sarcastically or in a straightforward manner, His words in Luke 15:7 proves the point of this appendix. There are people who are righteous in their experience. Such people "need no repentance." While we might debate whether the ninety-nine refer to righteous people,[1] the Lord does indicate that righteous people do not need to repent.

Some may object that none is righteous (Rom 3:10). However, that is only true in terms of man apart from God's intervention.

Believers are righteous in their standing before God by virtue of faith in Christ. That is what justification by faith alone means. "Abraham believed God and it was accounted to him for righteousness" (Rom 4:3). "But to him who does not work but believes on Him who justifies the ungodly, his faith is accounted for righteousness" (Rom 4:5).

But Luke, the same author who reported Luke 15:7, in his Gospel tells us of multiple people who were righteous *in their experience.* Luke mentions the soon-to-be parents of John the Baptist, Zacharias and

---
[1] See Appendix 1, note 1, for a discussion of whether the Lord was making a matter-of-fact comment or an ironic (or sarcastic) one.

Elizabeth (Luke 1:5) and then says, "they were both righteous before God, walking in all the commandments and ordinances of the Lord blameless" (Luke 1:6). Note that this is not imputed righteousness by faith. This is personal righteousness manifested in keeping God's commandments.

Similarly, in his second chapter, Luke tells us about Simeon saying, "this man was just [or righteous] and devout." The word used here is *dikaios*, the same word used in Luke 1:6 to refer to Elizabeth and Zacharias.

Dikaios is used by a centurion in Luke 23:47 when he said of the Lord Jesus Christ immediately after He breathed His last, "Certainly this was a righteous Man!"

The same word is used by other Biblical authors to refer to believers living righteously in their experience.[2] We find references to those who were righteous in their experience in Hebrews 11:4 (Abel), James 5:16 ("the effective, fervent prayer of a righteous man avails much"), 1 Peter 3:12 ("the eyes of the Lord are on the righteous"), 2 Peter 2:7-8 (Lot), and 1 John 3:12 ("Cain…murdered his brother…because his works were evil and his brother's righteous").

Repentance is for those who are not righteous in their experience. That is, it is for believers who are out of fellowship with God.

First John Does Not Mention Repentance

One year in the late nineties, the Grace Evangelical Society annual conference theme was repentance. During a question and answer time, I was asked a tough question:

> You conclude that since repentance is not found in John's Gospel, an evangelistic book, then repentance is not a condition of salvation. But what about First John? I know you believe, as I do, that its purpose is to lead believers to walk in fellowship with God. But First John does not mention repentance either.

---

[2] There is even one reference to an unbeliever who was said by his friends to have been living righteously. In Acts 10:22, those sent by Cornelius say that Cornelius is "a just [righteous, *dikaios*] man, one who fears God and has a good reputation among all the nation of the Jews." Of course, God does not call him righteous.

Aren't you forced to conclude, based on your own reasoning, that repentance is not a condition for fellowship with God?

I can't remember my answer. But I don't think I realized at the time how powerful this argument is. He was making a great point.

First John is written to mature believers, as 1 John 2:12-14 shows. These were people, likely elders in local churches, who were already in fellowship with God. Thus, the same reasoning indeed applies. Those in fellowship with God, those already living righteously, do not need to repent in order to remain in fellowship.

According to 1 John, the way the believer in fellowship with God maintains that fellowship is by walking in the light (1 John 1:7) and by confessing his sins (1 John 1:9). Confessing one's sins is not repentance.[3] It is agreeing with God that we now realize that we sinned. God uses confession to change us.

Paul Never Mentions Repentance for Those in Fellowship

As discussed in Appendix 2, Paul doesn't even mention repentance in ten of his epistles.[4] And in the other three he only mentions it five

---

[3] Some think that there is an element of repentance in confession. That is, they think that when we confess, we are also turning from the sin(s) which we are confessing. See, for example, "Repentance and Confession," by Charles Stanley (https://www.intouch.org/Read/Blog/repentance-and-confession). He writes, "Confession means agreeing with God that what we did was wrong. But that alone will not keep us from repeating it. That's why repentance should always be a part of confession." While this may seem correct, it is not Biblical language. We are never told in Scripture that repentance is a part of confession. Of course, confession is not the mouthing of words. To confess, we must agree with God. In a Bible study I was teaching, I heard a man who reported that when he was in high school he used to get drunk on Saturday nights each week. He planned it out. He had the idea that he would confess his sin Sunday morning and be right back in fellowship. The problem was that he was walking in the darkness, and he was not agreeing with God that what he did was wrong. Confession means you agree with God that what you did was wrong. But he did not think that what he did was wrong. He thought it was right. That was a young man out of fellowship with God. In fact, he reported that after a few months, he stopped going to church altogether because it was too hard to go to church after drinking until the wee hours of Sunday morning. It wasn't until he later repented that he got back to church and to fellowship with God. During the entire time of willful rebellion against God, he was out of fellowship, even though for a few months he formally admitted to God that he had been drunk. See Appendix 4 for more details.

[4] See Appendix 2, Reason #3.

times. And even then, he never indicates that repentance is a way for a believer to remain in fellowship with God.

All his epistles are designed to move believers to walk in fellowship with God. If repentance is the way to remain in fellowship with God, then why didn't Paul say so?

Evidence That Repentance Is a Condition to Restore Fellowship with God

Luke 15:1-31 Shows that Repentance Is for Those Who Stray

First Corinthians 13 is the love chapter. First Corinthians 15 is the resurrection chapter. Luke 15 is the repentance chapter.

Luke 15 features three parables, each of which deals with repentance. There is the Parable of the Lost Sheep (Luke 15:4-7), the Parable of the Lost Coin (Luke 15:8-10), and the Parable of the Lost Son (Luke 15:11-32). In all three parables what is lost was not originally lost.

The sheep that strayed away was originally safely in the fold with the other ninety-nine sheep under the care and protection of the shepherd.

The coin that was lost was originally with the other nine coins (probably on a bracelet).

The son who went into the far country was originally in fellowship with his Father.

The sheep that strayed did not become a member of the flock by returning. It returned to the experience it had before it strayed. The coin did not suddenly become a coin after it was found. It returned to its former place. The son did not become a son by returning. He was a son before he left, while he was in the far country, and when he returned. What changed was his fellowship with his father. While in the far country he was out of fellowship. His father put it this way, "this my son was dead and is alive again; he was lost and is found" (Luke 15:24). Notice the word *again*. In the past the son had been *alive* to his father in the sense that he had enjoyed fellowship with him. While in the far country, his son was *dead* to him. They were not in fellowship. When he returned, he was *again alive*, again in fellowship with his father.[5]

---

[5] The Lord does not tell us what the sins of the prodigal son were. The older brother says he spent his money on harlots (verse 30). But that is not found in the Lord's narration of the

No Repentance Verses Deal with Believers in Fellowship

As mentioned above, there are nineteen verses which refer to believers *who are out of fellowship with God* and who need to repent. None of the nineteen deal with believers who are walking in fellowship with God.

Revelation 2-3 Shows that Repentance Is to Restore Fellowship

Eight of the nineteen repentance verses that deal with believers out of fellowship are found in Revelation 2-3. These are in the seven letters to seven churches. In each case believers who are out of fellowship with God are called upon to repent (Rev 2:5, twice, 16, 21, twice, 22; 3:3, 19). Two of the seven churches, Smyrna (Rev 2:8-11) and Philadelphia (Rev 3:7-13), are good churches, that is, churches in fellowship with God. Repentance is not mentioned in the letters to those two churches.

The five churches which are not walking in fellowship with God are called upon to repent. The two churches already walking in fellowship with God are not.

Other Teaching about Believers Straying or Wandering

There is a recurring theme that runs from the Gospels through the Epistles concerning believers who stray. This theme is well known in Evangelicalism. It is sometimes calling *backsliding*.

However, what is not well known in Evangelicalism is that only believers who have strayed need to repent. Believers who are walking in the light of God's Word (1 John 1:7) and confessing their sins (1 John 1:9) do not need to repent because they have not strayed.

We saw this in the three parables of Luke 15. Who needed to repent? The sheep that strayed, the coin that was lost, and the son who went into the far country.

On multiple occasions the Lord Jesus said, "Those who are well have no need of a physician, but those who are sick. I have not come to call the righteous [*dikaious*, from *dikaios*], but sinners, to repentance" (Luke

---

story and is quite likely something made up by the older brother. The text vaguely says that he "wasted his possessions with prodigal living" (verse 3). The Lord is not concerned to give examples of the sins he committed while *dead to his father*. Whatever his sins were, he represents a believer who rebelled against God and then "came to himself" (verse 17, i.e., he came to his senses). Meanwhile, God was ready and waiting to take him back into fellowship.

5:32//Matt 9:13//Mark 2:17). That is the same point He made in Luke 15:7. The righteous do not need to repent. Repentance is for those who are not righteous, that is, for those who have strayed (Luke 15:4-6).[6]

Elizabeth and Zacharias did not need to repent. They were walking in fellowship with God. Simeon did not need to repent. Nor did Elijah (Jas 5:16-18) or anyone who was walking in fellowship with God.

In both of his letters to Timothy, Paul talked about believers who strayed (1 Tim 1:6; 6:10, 21; 2 Tim 2:18). He was telling Timothy to warn the believers in Ephesus not to stray.

James spoke of believers who wander: "Brethren, if anyone among you wanders from the truth, and someone turns him back, let him know that he who turns a sinner from the error of his way will save a soul [or, life] from death and cover a multitude of sins" (Jas 5:19–20). Notice that believers ("anyone among you," that is, among the "brethren") who wander need to be turned back or else they will ultimately experience premature death. Those who help them *turn back* are getting them *to repent*. Those who wander need to repent.

James did not call for believers to turn back other believers who have not wandered. A person can only turn back to the Lord if he has wandered away. One who is in fellowship with God, that is, one who is righteous, cannot turn back to the Lord. If he were to turn, he would be turning *away from the Lord.*

Conclusion

I find it quite motivating and encouraging to realize that God loves me and fellowships with me even though I am a sinful man. As long as my heart is set on Him, I walk in fellowship with Him even though I mess up.

---

[6] There is no verse which indicates precisely at what point one has strayed. If a person misses church on one Sunday, he has not yet strayed unless the reason he missed was that he decided to depart from Christian fellowship. But if a person misses church for months and months, he has likely strayed. Fellowship with God is tied with our fellowship with other righteous believers (cf. 1 John 1:3-4). In other words, church and the Lord's Supper are intimately tied with fellowship with God. In terms of confession of sins, I see no evidence in Scripture that a person falls out of fellowship every time he sins. As I understand 1 John 1:7 and 1 John 1:9, as long a believer walks in the light and confesses his sins when he becomes aware of them, he remains in fellowship.

What I mean by having my heart set on Him is that I want to please Him, and therefore, I am open and honest with Him, confessing my sins as I realize them (cf. 1 John 1:6-10).

If I thought I had to repent all day long, I'd want to lay out what the rules are. How do I repent when I already love God and wish to please Him? How much remorse do I need to demonstrate? When can I know I'm back in fellowship?

I rejoice that the Christian life is relatively simple. God loves me. Because I focus on that, I love Him back. I want to please Him. I wake up wanting to please Him. Now, I fail. A lot. But there is comfort in knowing that the blood of Jesus cleanses me from all sin (1 John 1:7), as long as I confess the sins of which I'm aware (1 John 1:9).

It is comforting to me to think that I've been walking in fellowship with God for years. If I thought I never walked in fellowship with Him more than a few hours (since the last time I repented), I'd be discouraged. I delight in a Lord who loves me. I bet you do too.

APPENDIX 4

How We Can Have Assurance That We Are in Fellowship with God

WHAT IS THE RELATIONSHIP between confession, repentance, and fellowship with God? What precisely must one do to have and maintain that fellowship? How does a born-again person know that he is currently in fellowship with God?

God has given us some broad principles to give us assurance that we are in fellowship with Him. The first four principles are essential to being in fellowship with God. Someone can follow one, two, or even three of these principles and yet not be in fellowship. All four are needed. The fifth principle concerns assurance that we are experiencing *mature fellowship* with God.

Principle #1: Loving God Is Vital to Fellowship with Him (1 John 1:4; 4:19)

First, you must love God to be in fellowship with Him. The Lord Jesus indicated that the greatest commandment is this: "You shall love the Lord your God with all your heart, with all your soul, and with all your mind" (Deut 6:4; Matt 22:37//Mark 12:30).[1]

The word *fellowship* (Greek, *koinōnia*) has the basic sense of *sharing*. When we *fellowship* with other Christians, we are sharing experiences

---

[1] Those who fulfill this command are in fellowship with God. But I list this as one of four essential principles because love for God is quite subjective. It is possible to have great affection for God and yet not truly love Him (e.g., the scribes and Pharisees). It is also possible to wonder if you love God *with your whole heart, soul, mind, and strength,* when in fact, you do (e.g., perfectionists). One who truly loves God walks in the light, confesses his sins, and fellowships with other believers. Those later principles are less subjective.

with them (a meal, worship, prayer, etc.). Fellowship is a relational term. When we are *in fellowship* with God, we share His way of looking at life (principle #2), and we recognize that our life is lived in communion with Him. His Spirit energizes and motivates us. One of the central motivations for a believer in fellowship is love for God. John said, "We love Him because He first loved us" (1 John 4:19). As he reflected on Christ's death for us, Paul said that "the love of Christ constrains us" (2 Cor 5:14).

If a believer does *not* love God, then he is *not* in fellowship with God.[2] Almost everyone in Christendom recognizes that fact.

However, the opposite is not true. The fact that someone loves Jesus does not mean that he is necessarily in fellowship with Him. It is possible to have great love for Jesus and a strong desire to please Him and yet promote works salvation (or other false teachings), not confess one's sins, and not assemble each week with other believers.

Principle #2: Walking in the Light Is Necessary for Fellowship (1 John 1:3-4, 7)

Second, fellowship with God requires *walking in the light,* as opposed to walking in the darkness. Hodges suggests that "to walk in the light must mean essentially to live in God's presence, exposed to what He has revealed about Himself. This, of course, is done through openness in prayer and through openness to the Word of God in which He is revealed."[3] In many spheres of Evangelicalism today there is an anti-doctrinal sentiment. Many Evangelicals think that doctrine is bad since it can divide people. Therefore, many put an emphasis—or the entire emphasis—on loving God (principle #1).

But Scripture shows that only those who "walk in the light" (as opposed to walking in darkness) are in fellowship with God. Only then does "the blood of Jesus cleanse us from all sin" (1 John 1:5-7).

---

[2] It is difficult to know that we love God *with all our heart, all our soul, all our mind, and all our strength.* The way in which we measure ourselves against this command is by asking questions like, "Do I desire God's will to be done in my life? Do I want to please Him? Do I long for His approval?" Since Scripture does not give us any way to quantify our love for God, it is unwise to speculate concerning our degree of love for God. We are to live by faith. In addition, we have other principles to guide us as to whether we are in fellowship. That is why I say that all four of these principles are required.

[3] Zane C. Hodges, *The Epistles of John* (Irving, TX: Grace Evangelical Society, 1999), p. 61.

God's Word is to be a light unto our path if we are walking in fellowship with God (Ps 119:105). Walking in the light is to bring our lives under the spotlight of God's Word.

That means, of course, that we must regularly be exposed to the teachings of God's Word. Typically, that occurs in our local church (see principle #4),[4] though today most people have the Bible in their own languages and can supplement the teaching they receive with personal Bible reading.

Part of walking in the light is continuing to believe *the core doctrines* of the Christian faith. The core doctrines include the deity of Christ, the virgin birth, substitutionary atonement, Jesus' bodily resurrection, and justification by faith alone, apart from works. Some would include the inerrancy of Scripture as a fundamental truth. If a person rejects any fundamental doctrine, then he is not in fellowship with God (cf. 2 Cor 11:3; Gal 1:6-9; 1 Tim 1:18-20; 4:16; 2 Tim 2:16-18; Titus 1:9).

We should not confuse walking in the light with obeying His commandments (compare 1 John 1:7 and 1 John 2:3-11). John is speaking of the mature believer when he refers to those who obey His commandments (1 John 2:3-11). A brand-new believer can walk in the light, even though he does not yet know or apply most of the commandments.

The second greatest commandment, loving your neighbor as yourself (Matt 22:39//Mark 12:31), falls under principle #2 (as well as principles #3-5). Anyone walking in the light is loving his neighbors (1 John 3:16-18; 4:20).

Principle #3: Confessing Our Sins
Is Required for Fellowship (1 John 1:9)

Third, one must confess his sins. The issue of confession is rather fuzzy for most Evangelicals. Is it enough to acknowledge to God that I am a sinner and I've sinned this week? Many churches have public readings where the entire congregation confesses their sinfulness.

There is no indication in 1 John 1:9 that a weekly confession at church is what God has in mind. Certainly, it is fine to confess our

---

[4] In his discussion of 1 John 1:7, I. Howard Marshall says concerning those who walk in the light that "persons who cut themselves off from fellowship with other Christians cannot have fellowship with God" (*The Epistles of John* [Grand Rapids, MI: Eerdmans, 1978], pp. 111-12).

sinfulness at church. But God wants us to be open and honest about our sin as soon as we recognize it.

King David said, "When I kept silent my bones wasted away all day long" (Ps 32:3). He was talking about the time, nearly a year, after he committed adultery and murder. He kept silent about his sin, and he was in pain all day long. Only when he confessed his sin to God did he experience God's forgiveness: "I acknowledged my sin to You…and you forgave the iniquity of my sin" (Ps 32:5; see also 2 Sam 12:1-15, esp. verse 13, "I have sinned against the Lord").

According to 1 John 1:9, our forgiveness and cleansing are conditioned upon our confession of our sins as we become aware of them ("If we confess…"). Therefore, we not only confess the general fact that we sin and fall short of God's glory (Rom 3:23), but we also confess the specific sins of which we become aware (cf. 2 Sam 12:7, 13; Ps 32:3-5; Prov 28:13). I. Howard Marshall says, "To confess sins is not merely to admit that we are sinners, but to lay them before God and to seek forgiveness."[5] Similarly Smalley says, "The use of the plural, 'sins' (*tas hamartias*), probably indicates that the confession of particular acts of sin is meant in the context, rather than the acknowledgement of 'sin' in general."[6] A century earlier Westcott wrote that the confession "extends to specific, definite acts, and not only to sin in general terms."[7]

The other contextual indication that specific sins are to be confessed is the expression "all unrighteousness." God *forgives us our sins*, the sins we confess, and *cleanses us from all unrighteousness*. While many commentators see these expressions as synonymous,[8] the word *all* before *unrighteousness* suggests otherwise. Hodges says that *all unrighteousness* "is broader and covers any latent attitude or outlook that is sinful in

---

[5] Marshall, *The Epistles of John*, p. 113.
[6] Stephen S. Smalley, *1, 2, 3 John* (Waco, TX: Word Books, 1984), p. 31. See also Gary Derickson, *1, 2, & 3 John* (Bellingham, WA: Lexham Press, 2014) who says that "This form of confession is heartfelt and *consciously specific*…it is the confession involving naming particular sins" (p. 108, emphasis added).
[7] Brooke Foss Westcott, *The Epistles of St. John* (Grand Rapids, MI: Eerdmans, 1883, 1885, 1892, 1966), p. 24.
[8] See, for example, Raymond E. Brown, *The Epistles of John* (Garden City, NY: Doubleday, 1982), p. 211. See also Marshall, who says, "Most commentators regard the two terms [forgive sins and cleanse all unrighteousness] as synonymous," *The Epistles of John*, p. 114. However, Marshall suggests it is possible that the cleansing is a bit broader than forgiveness and "signifies the removal not only of the guilt of sin but also of the power of sin in the human heart."

character, whether or not it has found expression in overt sin...the cleansing that follows [confession of specific sins] *covers everything* that needs cleansing."[9] None of us can possibly confess all our sins. Hodges says, "No one but God can ever possibly know the full extent of our sinfulness, so that we can only actually confess the sins of which we are aware. God does not ask more of us than that."[10] The sins which we confess are but the tip of the iceberg.

There is no special prayer of confession of specific sins given in Scripture.[11] The words of the Lord's prayer, "forgive us our trespasses as we forgive those who trespass against us," are general in nature. What God is looking for is for us to be honest with Him.

Confessing the sins of which we are aware is a vital aspect of fellowship with God.[12]

Principle #4: Going to Church Is Essential for Fellowship with God (Acts 2:42; Hebrews 10:23-25)

Fourth, one must gather with other believers regularly. While we may respect and admire ascetics who spent years in isolation in a cave, the truth is that asceticism does not work (see, for example, Col 2:20-23). Fellowship with God occurs in a corporate context, not in isolation.

The local church is the place in which believers are to gather and encourage one another until Christ returns (Heb 10:23-25). To forsake such assembling together is to violate a crucial fellowship principle.

---

[9] Hodges, *The Epistles of John*, p. 65. Derickson seems to take the same position when he says that "This first promise covers only those [sins] confessed" and that "Second, God cleanses us, makes us morally pure" (*1, 2, & 3 John*, p. 111). See also David R. Anderson, *Maximum Joy: First John—Relationship or Fellowship?* (Irving, TX: Grace Evangelical Society, 2005), p. 55. Anderson says, "'All unrighteousness' refers to all the rest of the sinfulness and/or sins I do not know about, that is, ones I do not see."
[10] Hodges, *The Epistles of John*, p. 65.
[11] Smalley, "The manner of the acknowledgement is not specified," *1, 2, 3 John*, p. 31.
[12] John MacArthur, commenting on 1 John 1:9, says, "We've already discussed the difference between judicial and parental forgiveness—the latter is in view in 1 John 1:9. It is a subjective, relational kind of forgiveness. It is the restoration to a place of blessing in the eyes of a displeased father. Similarly, the cleansing of 1 John 1:9 doesn't refer to regeneration. Rather, it is a spiritual washing to rid you of the defilement caused by sin in your daily walk. The verse is speaking of an ongoing pardon and purification from sin, not the cleansing and forgiveness of salvation" (https://www.oneplace.com/ministries/grace-to-you/read/articles/if-we-confess-our-sins-9344.html).

I realize that some today have difficulty finding a solid Bible teaching church close to them. In that case I'd suggest moving to a place where there is one. If that is not feasible, then gather with your family for the Lord's Supper, prayer, and a message from God's Word each week.[13]

Some people treat their home Bible study as church. If you were to add in the Lord's Supper and baptism, that study becomes a home church.

I. Howard Marshall says, "Persons who cut themselves off from fellowship with other Christians cannot have fellowship with God."[14]

The early church in Jerusalem was growing steadily. Luke says, "And they continued steadfastly in the apostles' doctrine and fellowship, in the breaking of bread [i.e., the Lord's Supper], and in prayers" (Acts 2:42). Fellowship with God flourishes in a context where people regularly receive the teaching of apostolic doctrine, where the Lord's Supper is presented, and where prayers are uplifted.

Principle #5: Living Righteously Demonstrates Mature Fellowship (1 Corinthians 2:14–3:3; 1 John 2:3-11)

Fifth, mature fellowship with God manifests itself in a holy life. Many Evangelicals equate fellowship with God with Christian maturity. In that view immature Christians are not in fellowship with God. Only mature Christians are in fellowship with God.

That would mean that all new believers, who are by definition "babes in Christ" and not yet spiritual believers (1 Cor 2:14–3:3), are out of

---

[13] The New Testament does not tell us what to do if there is not a solid Bible-teaching church in your area. We know from the last chapter of Romans that there were at least fifteen different house churches in Rome (cf. Rom 16:3, 5, 6, 7, 8, 9, 10 twice, 11 twice, 12 twice, 13, 14, 15). Some of these were so small that they are called *tenement churches* (which met in rooms about 10 feet by 10 feet). See Robert Jewett, *Romans: A Commentary,* ed. Eldon Jay Epp, Hermeneia (Minneapolis, MN: Fortress, 2007), pp. 55-88. Paul implies that all these churches were sound. However, Galatians shows Paul clearly did not want believers listening to the message of Judaizers. Likewise, 1 John is clear that believers are not to listen to the false teachers known as antichrists. At the time the New Testament Epistles were written, these false teachers evidently did not have actual churches. They simply traveled and taught. But today we have lots of towns, even in the United States, especially in rural areas, where there is no church proclaiming the promise of everlasting life that can never be lost. Based on Galatians and 1 John, if the only options in your town are churches proclaiming the idea that salvation can be lost, the application would be to start your own house church or move to a city with a solid church.

[14] Marshall, *The Epistles of John,* pp. 111-12.

fellowship with God. But that is incorrect. A new believer begins the Christian life in fellowship with God (Acts 10:43). If he continues to love God, walk in the light, confess his sins, and learn about Christ at church, he remains in fellowship with God, even though he is spiritually immature.[15]

There is a subtle distinction in 1 John between being *in fellowship with God* (1 John 1:6-10) and *knowing God* in our experience (1 John 2:3-11). Only the mature believer knows God experientially. Hodges explains the distinction in this way, "Just as a claim to fellowship with Him is false if we 'walk in darkness,' so too a disobedient lifestyle falsifies any claim to intimate knowledge of Him."[16]

Can You Answer These Questions Affirmatively?

Based on the five principles given above, we can generate some fellowship questions. Answer the first four positively, and you know you are in fellowship. If you can also answer question five affirmatively, then your fellowship with God is mature. Here are the key fellowship questions:

1. Do you believe fundamental Bible doctrine?
2. Do you love God and wish to please Him?
3. Do you confess your sins to God?
4. Do you fellowship with other believers each week?
5. Do you manifest a transformed life?

I realize that some would say that if a person is not yet manifesting significant transformation in his life, then he cannot be in fellowship with God. However, Paul indicated that it is not surprising for "babes in Christ" to continue to live like unbelievers live until they have had enough time to grow (1 Cor 3:1-3). So, for the first year or so, a believer is a baby Christian. He is in fellowship with God if he walks in the

---

[15] Sadly, it is possible for a believer to remain in spiritual infancy for years or even decades. Even ongoing spiritual immaturity does not mean that one is out of fellowship with God. If he is fulfilling the four principles essential to fellowship, he remains in fellowship, even though his growth is stunted.

[16] Zane C. Hodges, *The Epistles of John: Walking in the Light of God's Love* (Irving, TX: Grace Evangelical Society, 1999), p. 77.

light, loves God, confesses his sins, and fellowships weekly with other believers. But spiritual maturity is yet future for him.

If someone has been a believer for four or five years, as the Corinthians had been when Paul wrote 1 Corinthians (the first word in the Greek text of 1 Cor 3:3 is *eti*, *still*, "for you are still carnal"), and he is still in spiritual diapers, then his growth has been stunted. That does not necessarily mean that he is out of fellowship with God. He is culpable for his continued spiritual immaturity. But he may love God, walk in the light, confess his sins, and assemble regularly with other believers.

Conclusion

I have not mentioned repentance thus far in this appendix. That is because believers only need to repent if they depart from fellowship with God (see Appendix 3).[17] For the believer who is in fellowship with God, he needs to walk in the light, love God, confess his sins, and assemble regularly with other believers in order to stay in fellowship with God. Repentance only comes into play if he turns away from the Lord (cf. Luke 15:11-24; Jas 5:19-20).

If you are a perfectionist, you may have trouble with the ambiguities in what I wrote above. What is the full list of fundamental doctrines I must believe to be in fellowship? How do I know if I'm loving God with my whole heart, soul, and mind? Do I confess my sins in the right way? Am I attending the right church?

If you are struggling with questions like these, I would encourage you to realize that God is not out to trip us up. He loves us and wants us to be in fellowship with Him. He has not made it difficult to know if we are in fellowship with Him.

But the second thing you should realize is this: God has given each local church a group of men whose job is to oversee the spiritual

---

[17] Hodges, commenting on confession in 1 John 1:9, says, "It should be noted that the word *repentance* is not used here, nor anywhere in the epistle. The reason for this is simple. In John's usage, Christian repentance is appropriate when a pattern of sin is persisted in and needs to be changed (see Revelation 2:5, 16, 21, 22; 3:3, 19). In our text, John is talking about those who *discover* sin while in fellowship with God, not those who have wandered away from Him or have lost some previous spiritual attainment. That is a separate issue. The audience of First John is spiritually stable and has nothing to repent of (see 2:12-14, 21). Their task is to 'abide,' or 'stay,' in Christ and His truth (see 2:24, 28), not to 'turn back' to Him" (*The Epistles of John*, p. 63, emphases his).

lives of the flock. These men are called *elders* or *overseers* in the New Testament. Maybe your church calls these people *pastors, deacons,* or *the board*. Whatever they are called, they are tasked with making sure that those who are members of the body are in fellowship with God. If they consider you a member in good standing, then they are saying that they believe you are in fellowship with God. If they permit you to partake of the Lord's Supper, and they do not exercise church discipline against you, then you can take comfort that someone external to you believes you are in fellowship with God.[18]

I was raised under a lot of perfectionism. When I came to faith, I found it hard to envision God loving me just as I was. Oh, *I knew He accepted me just as I was*. But for a time, I thought He must be dissatisfied with me as my earthly father was. Only as I matured in the faith did I realize that God the Father is not like my earthly father. I came to see that He was satisfied with the gradual progress I was making in the Christian life.

I'd love to be perfect right now. I bet you would too. But that day is yet future (1 John 3:2). Until then, let's walk in fellowship with God. Remember, fellowship with God is better than anything this world has to offer (Luke 15:11-32).

---

[18] Admittedly, there are many churches that do not practice church discipline except in the most extreme and obvious cases. So, the fact that the leaders in one's church accept a person as being in good standing with the Lord is not necessarily proof that he is. However, if the leaders practice church discipline and sometimes exclude certain believers from partaking in the Lord's Supper, then if they accept someone as being in good standing, that is meaningful.

APPENDIX 5

Faith Alone in One Hundred Verses

Lewis Sperry Chafer famously said there are over 150 verses in the New Testament that clearly say that everlasting life (or justification) is solely based upon a person's belief or faith in Jesus Christ.[1]

I have found the number is slightly lower, depending on how we count. Obviously, a passage which repeatedly refers to faith alone for regeneration could be counted as one passage or multiple verses. Examples include John 3:14-18; 4:10-26; 5:24-47; 6:26-58; 11:25-27; Romans 4:1-6; Galatians 3:6-14; 1 John 5:9-13.

There is even one verse, Galatians 2:16, which three times in the same verse says that justification is by faith and not by works. Is that one or three references? I counted it as one.

I have taken a sort of middle of the road approach to such passages, counting them as more than one in many cases, but often less than the number of verses involved.

If we are looking for texts that explicitly say that the one who believes in Jesus has everlasting life (or is saved or is justified), the number is around seventy-four.

If we include fifty-five texts which implicitly say that (for example, saying that someone is born again by the Word of God, but not specifically mentioning faith in Christ), the number rises to 129.

Note that in some of the seventy-four definite verses, faith is not specifically indicated as faith *in Christ*. Ephesians 2:8-9 is a famous example: "For by grace you have been saved [made alive, v 5] through faith…" Since in such cases it is clear based on the context that the author means faith in Christ, I have included these.

---

[1] Lewis Sperry Chafer, *Systematic Theology, Vol. 3* (Dallas, TX: Dallas Seminary Press, 1948), p. 376

Seventy-Four Verses Which Clearly Teach Faith Alone

Genesis has one: 15:6. In light of Genesis 15:1-5, John 8:56, Romans 4:3, and Galatians 3:6, this text is clearly teaches justification by faith alone in the coming Messiah, who is Jesus.

Matthew and Mark have no verses which explicitly teach faith alone.

Luke has one explicit verse on faith alone: 8:12, "The devil comes and takes away the word out of their hearts, lest they should believe and be saved."

John has at least eighteen clear texts on faith alone, though the number could realistically be much higher: 1:12; 3:15, 16, 18, 36; 4:10-14, 25-28; 5:24, 39-40; 6:35, 37, 39-40, 47; 10:24-30; 11:25, 26; 12:36, 46-47 (cf. v 50); 20:31.

Acts has seven clear faith-alone texts: 10:43 (compare Acts 11:14); 11:17; 13:39; 15:9, 11; 16:31; 26:18.

Romans has nineteen: 3:22, 24, 26, 27, 28, 30; 4:3, 5, 9, 11, 13, 16, 22, 24; 5:1; 9:30, 33; 10:4, 10 ("For with the heart one believes unto righteousness [=justification]").

First Corinthians has only one clear verse: 1:21, "to save those who believe."

Second Corinthians has two clear texts: 5:1-5, 8.

Galatians has a dozen clear texts: 2:16 ("justified…by faith in Jesus Christ"); 3:2, 5, 6, 7, 8, 9, 11, 14, 22, 24, 26.

Ephesians has two clear texts: 1:13; 2:8 (compare 2:5).

Philippians has one clear text on faith alone: 3:9 ("the righteousness which is from God by faith").

First Thessalonians has one: 5:10 ("whether we watch or sleep, we should live together with Him").

First Timothy has one: 1:16, "I [am]…a pattern to those who are going to believe on Him for everlasting life."

Second Timothy has two clear texts: 1:12 (Paul knows he will be with the Lord and will be rewarded by Him for the work he has done); 3:15.

Hebrews has three: 4:3; 10:10, 14. First John has two texts that clearly teach faith alone: 5:1, 9-13.

A few of those seventy-four do not explicitly mention faith in Christ. However, the context brings that out, so I included them. See

2 Corinthians 5:1-5, 8; 1 Thessalonians 5:10; Hebrews 10:10, 14, as examples.

If we were to be very narrow in our list, the number would be around sixty-nine.

Fifty-Five Implicit Faith Alone Verses

Matthew, Mark, and Luke have six implicit faith alone messages. In all six places the Lord Jesus, after healing someone, says, "your faith has saved you." Those verses are Matthew 9:22; Mark 5:34; 10:52; Luke 8:48; 17:19; 18:42. The Lord might have simply been referring to physical healing. However, it is quite possible that He was referring to both physical healing and eternal salvation.

John has fifteen implicit faith alone texts: 1:7; 2:23; 4:39, 41, 42; 6:29; 7:38-39; 8:24, 30-31; 11:15; 14:6; 17:20, 21; 19:35; 20:29.

Acts has nineteen possible implicit faith alone texts: 3:16; 4:4, 12; 8:12, 13 (compare v 17); 9:42; 11:14, 21; 14:1, 23, 27; 15:7; 17:4, 12; 18:8, 27; 19:4; 20:21; 21:25.

Romans has one: 11:6.

Second Corinthians has one: 4:4.

Galatians has one: 2:21.

Philippians also has one: 1:29.

First Thessalonians has three implicit: 1:7; 2:10; 4:14.

Second Thessalonians has two: 1:10; 2:12.

First Timothy has one implicit verse: 4:10

Titus has one: 3:5-8.

James has two: 1:18; 2:23.

First Peter has one: 1:23.

And Revelation has one implicit text: 22:17.

If you have time, work your way through both lists. You might not agree on each and every one of the verses I listed there. You may have many more you put on your own list. But the point is clear. *There are a lot of verses in the Bible which make it crystal clear that justification/ regeneration/eternal salvation is gained simply by believing in the Lord Jesus Christ.* No works required. He took away the sin of the world at Calvary (John 1:29). All that we need to do is believe in Him in order to have the life which He promises to the believer, ever-lasting life.

Why Is There Resistance to This?

The puzzling question, in light of the evidence cited above, is why anyone in Christianity would deny that justification is by faith alone, apart from works? And why would anyone who calls himself a Christian say that we are justified by faith alone, but then define true faith as including repentance, commitment, and obedience?

The faith-alone message is hard to believe. That is the bottom line. And many if not most people in Christianity are unwilling to believe it.

I personally was opposed to this message and unwilling to believe it until one day before my senior year in college a friend, John Carlson, asked me if my view of the gospel might be wrong. That hit me hard. At that moment I became willing to consider whether I was wrong. I told the Lord that. But I also told Him that I had to be convinced by the Bible. After five one-hour sessions debating the faith-alone message with a Cru staff member, Warren Wilke, I came to faith in Christ for everlasting life. I knew I had everlasting life by faith alone and that I could never lose it. What a day of rejoicing that was.

In His ministry in Israel, Jesus repeatedly confronted this very situation of legalists unwilling to believe. Here is one of my favorite texts on that issue, one of the definite verses listed above, John 5:39-40. The Lord said, "You search the Scriptures, for in them you think you have eternal life; and these are they which testify of Me. But you are not willing to come to Me that you may have life."

Do you believe? That is, are you convinced that all who simply believe in Jesus for everlasting life have that life?

If not, are you willing to believe that?

Is it possible your view of the gospel is wrong?

I am so thankful for the witness of John Carlson and Warren Wilke. They convinced me that the faith-alone message is correct. You might say that I'm *eternally grateful*.

Scripture Index

Genesis
- 3:4 63
- 6:1-8 74
- 15:6 .... 32, 94
- 15:16 74

Exodus
- 33:32 49
- 34:9 25

Leviticus
- 26 22
- 26:40-45 31

Numbers
- 14:19-20 25
- 23:19 21
- 30:5-13 25

Deuteronomy
- 4:25-31 31
- 6:4 121
- 28 22
- 29:19-20 25
- 30:1-10 31

2 Samuel
- 12:1-15 .... 25, 124
- 12:7, 13 124

2 Kings
- 24:4 25

2 Chronicles
- 7:14 25

Psalms
- 25:11 25
- 32:3 124
- 32:3-5 124
- 51 25
- 103:3 25
- 119:105 123

Proverbs
- 28:13 124

Isaiah
- 30:15 21
- 55:7 24

Jeremiah
- 3:12-18 31
- 18:1-11 31
- 21:9, 16; 21
- 31:31-34 32
- 50:4 21

Ezekiel
- 3:19 22
- 18 .... 23, 94
- 18:23 .... 22, 76
- 18:32 22
- 33:11 22

Daniel
- 7:22 35

Hosea
- 13:14 21
- 14:2 21

Amos
7:2 25

Jonah
3 ..... 24, 76
3:4 23
3:5-10 ..... 23, 24, 29, 30, 48
3:10 ..... 23, 29, 102
4:11 23

Zechariah
12:10 32

Matthew
2:3 41
3:2 ..... 9, 30, 32, 33, 37, 103
3:2; 4:17 ..... 30, 100, 110
3:2, 8, 11 113
3:5 41
3:6 30
4:17 ..... 9, 30, 32, 33, 37, 103, 113
9:13 ..... 101, 103, 114
9:28 106
11:20, 21 ..... 30, 113
12:41 ..... 24, 29, 30, 48, 102, 113
22:37 121
23:37-39 ..... 31, 32
22:39 123
24:1-2 41
24:21-22 74
27:3 28
28:18-20 49

Mark
1:4 ..... 50, 114
1:14-15 ..... 36, 110
1:15 ..... 10, 100, 113
2:17 ..... 101, 114
6:12 ..... 101, 113
6:12-13 103
12:30 121
12:31 123
16:15 49
16:15-16 49
16:16 18

Luke
1:5 115
1:6 115
1:16 28
3:3 50
3:3, 8 114
5:32 ..... 47, 101, 114
10:13 113
11:32 113
13:1 39
13:1-5 ..... 39, 42
13:3 47
13: 3, 5 110
13:3-5 9
13:3, 5 ..... 41, 50, 100, 113
13:4 40
15:1-31 117
15:1-32 29
15:4-6 119
15:4-7 117
15:7 ..... 101, 103, 114
15:7, 10 78
15:8-10 117
15:11-19 91
15:11-24 ..... 42, 70, 90, 95, 128
15:11-32 ..... 91, 117, 129
15:17 67
15:20-32 91
15:24 117
16:19-31 ..... 10, 45, 110
16:29 45
16:29, 31 46
16:30 ..... 10, 100
16:30-31 46
16:31 ..... 44, 45
17:3-4 50
17:3, 4 114
19:43-44 41
22:32 28
23:47 115
24:27 114
24:47 ..... 10, 47, 48, 49, 52, 100, 110

John
1:7 50

Scripture Index

Reference	Pages
1:11	41
1:11-13	32
1:35-40	85
2:24	106
3:3, 5	37
3:5	23
3:8b-9	23
3:14-18	24, 73
3:16	72, 73, 85, 87, 89, 91, 102, 108
3:16-17	75
3:17-18	73
3:36	50
4:16	86
5:24	24, 51, 72
6:28-29	102
6:28-29, 47	24
6:47	72
8:24	106
8:54-59	32
11:25-27	24, 106
11:26	91
11:27	107
13:9-11	48
13:10	48
16:8	86
20:21-23	49
20:23	48
20:30-31	108
20:31	54, 106

Acts

Reference	Pages
1:6-8	49
2:36	55
2:37	55
2:38	9, 18, 48, 49, 50, 51, 53, 54, 55, 56, 57, 58, 100, 110, 114
2:42	125, 126
3:19	51, 101, 103, 113
3:26	28
4:12	46
5:31	50, 51, 113
7:54	55
7:57	55
7:60	49
8:10	96
8:12	106
8:12-13	57
8:13	50, 107
8:14-17	56
8:15	57
8:16-17	57
8:22	29, 49, 50, 51, 107, 114
8:22-23	96
8:36-37	18
9:6	56
9:17-18	56
9:26	106
9:35	28
10	56
10:1-8	70
10-11	10
10:43	48, 49, 52, 63, 75, 96, 127
10:45	61
11:1	61
11:2	59, 61
11:14	49, 70
11:18	10, 51, 61, 62, 63, 100, 102, 110, 114
13:24	51, 113
13:26-48	79
13:38-39	48, 49, 51
13:39	52, 103
13:46, 48	67
14:15	52, 79
15:1	61
15:5	61
15:5, 7	52
15:7-11	49, 52, 62, 63, 75, 76
15:9	52
15:19	28, 52
16:30	55, 79, 102
16:30-31	52, 89
16:31	51, 57, 72, 79, 103
17:4, 5, 12, 34	52
17:11	11, 13
17:30	18, 29, 51, 78, 104, 114
17:31	51, 78
17:34	51
18:8, 27	52

19:1, 4, 8-9	51	7:9, 10	67, 81, 114
19:4	10, 50, 51, 113	7:10	10, 29, 65, 67, 104, 109, 110
20:20-21	101	11:3	123
20:21	51, 80, 103, 114	12:21	67, 81, 109, 114
22:10	56		
22:16	48, 49, 56		
26:15	56		
26:18	52		
26:19-20	101		
26:20	51, 104		

Galatians

1:6-9	123
1:11-12	56
2:3-5	61
2:7	106
2:14-21	59
2:16	51, 67, 79, 108
3:5-14	108
3:6-14	51
3:9-11	61
5:2-4, 7-12	61
6:12-15	61
6:16	32

Romans

2:1-3	81
2:4	10, 67, 80, 81, 109, 114
3:11	114
3:21—4:25	81
3:21-31	67
3:22, 25, 26, 27, 28, 30	108
3:23	124
4:3	114
4:4-5	79
4:5	114
6:8	106
10:14-17	18
11:26	28
12:1-2	70, 91
14:13-14	16

Ephesians

2:5, 8	67
2:8-9	51, 57, 79, 89, 108
2:9	102

Philippians

1:3-11	72

Colossians

1:13-14	48
2:20-23	125

1 Corinthians

2:14—3:3	126
2:16	91
3:1-3	127
3:3	128
9:17	106
11:7	71
15:1-11	35

1 Thessalonians

1:2-10	69
1:9	10, 69, 72, 100, 110
2:4	106
4:13-18	69
4:14	106

2 Corinthians

2:4-5	65
2:6-11	65
3:18	70, 91
5:14	122
5:19-20	75
7:8	65
7:8-10	65
7:9	109

1 Timothy

1:6	119
1:11	106
1:16	51, 67, 108
1:18-20	123
2:4	76
2:4-5	75
4:16	123
6:10, 21	119

Scripture Index

2 Timothy
- 2:16-18 123
- 2:18 119
- 2:24-26 .... 101, 104
- 2:25 .... 81, 109, 114

Titus
- 1:2 67
- 1:3 106
- 1:9 123
- 3:7 67

Hebrews
- 6:1, 6 114
- 6:4-5 10
- 6:4-8 82
- 6:6 81
- 6:7-8 82
- 10:17-18 48
- 10:23-25 .... 96, 125
- 11:6 .... 18, 106
- 12:17 114

James
- 3:9 71
- 5:16 115
- 5:16-18 119
- 5:19-20 .... 82, 91, 119, 128
- 5:20 28

1 Peter
- 1:21-24 75
- 1:23-25 76
- 2:9 18
- 2:25 28
- 3:12 115

2 Peter
- 2:7-8 115
- 3:1-8 74
- 3:1-13 73
- 3:6 74
- 3:9 .... 9, 32, 75, 76, 100, 110, 114

1 John
- 1:3-4 119
- 1:3-4, 7 122
- 1:5-7 122
- 1:6-10 .... 120, 127
- 1:7 .... 116, 118, 120, 123
- 1:7-9 .... 48, 95
- 1:9 .... 48, 90, 116, 118, 120, 123
- 2:3-11 .... 123, 126, 127
- 2:12-14 116
- 3:2 129
- 3:12 115
- 3:16-18 123
- 4:19 .... 121, 122
- 4:20 123
- 5:1 .... 54, 106

Revelation
- 2-3 118
- 2:5 .... 114, 118
- 2:8-11 118
- 2:16, 21 114
- 2:21 .... 29, 107
- 2:22 .... 29, 107
- 3:3, 19 .... 114, 118
- 3:7-13 .... 72, 118
- 3:10 72
- 7:1-8 32
- 9:20 29
- 9:20, 21 .... 75, 114
- 9:21 29
- 16:9, 11 .... 75, 114
- 16:11 29
- 22:17 .... 57, 72, 89

Subject Index

Abide 128
Abraham 10, 43-46, 110, 114
Apostasy... 82
Aproval... 122
Arminius.. 16
Assembly.. 99
Assurance 6, 11, 78, 121
Atonement... 123
Backsliding 118
Baptismal regeneration 53
Believe 5, 10-14, 16, 18-19, 24, 28,
    31-32, 35-36, 41, 45-46, 50-54, 57, 60,
    62, 65-66, 69, 76, 79-80, 85, 88-89, 91,
    93, 95, 100-102, 105-108, 112, 115,
    123, 127-129, 132-134
Birth 12, 48, 53-54, 87, 92-93, 96, 99,
    102, 104, 109-111, 123
Blood 39, 86, 120, 122
Bock, Darrell 40, 46, 54, 78-80, 103
Bread 126
Calvin, John................................... 65, 93
Carnal.. 69, 128
Certainty... 16
Children 23, 28, 89-90
Church 5, 7-8, 13-15,
    17-19, 24, 53, 57, 60, 65-67, 70, 72, 76,
    88, 90-91, 93, 95-96, 99-100, 108-109,
    116, 119, 123-129
Commitment...............11, 28-29, 88, 134
Communion....................................... 122
Confess...................... 18, 53, 89-90, 116,
    120, 122-125, 127-128
Confession................... 15-16, 18-19, 88,
    93, 95, 113, 116, 119, 121, 123-125,
    128
Confidence 28, 106
Conversion 17, 28, 71, 106
Cross................... 15, 48-49, 78-79, 88-89
Death.................. 15, 21-23, 25, 32, 35,
    40, 42, 48, 51, 55, 65-66, 73, 75-76, 78,
    82-83, 94, 101, 109-110, 119, 122
Death of Christ 15
Death on the cross 48, 78
Decision 29-30, 66, 95, 105
Deity.. 123
Disciple 14, 85
Discipleship 51, 58, 96, 104
Discipline............................. 65, 109, 129
Disobedience....................................... 25
Doubt 15-16, 32, 40
Drink 86
Elect 14, 74
Eternal rewards 82
Eternal security 57, 82
Evangelism.................................... 51, 79
Evangelizing 31, 108
Everlasting life................. 5, 9-12, 14-15,
    19, 21-25, 32-33, 37, 42, 45-47, 50-51,
    53-54, 56, 59-63, 65-67, 70-72, 77, 79,
    82-83, 85, 87-91, 93-96, 99-102, 104-
    105, 108-112, 114, 126, 131-132, 134
Faith.............................11, 14-18, 23, 28,

36, 42, 44, 48-57, 59-63, 66-67, 69-71, 76, 79-81, 86-92, 94-96, 99, 101-103, 105-109, 111, 114-115, 122-123, 129, 131-134
Faith alone 14, 16-17, 88, 90, 94, 102, 105, 114, 123, 131-134
Faithful 72
Fall away 81
Fellowship 6, 16, 19, 30, 37, 48-50, 61, 66, 70, 74, 78, 87, 90-91, 94-95, 104, 113-123, 125-129
Final judgment 40
Fire 75
Flesh 16, 74, 86
Follow 24, 35, 75, 86, 104, 121
Free Grace 11, 18, 85
Gospel 5, 8-11, 14-16, 18, 24, 32-33, 35-37, 48-49, 52, 56-57, 62, 72, 85-88, 94, 100, 102, 104, 108, 114-115, 118, 134
Grace 1-2, 11, 13-16, 18, 29, 31, 36, 57, 63, 73, 76, 79, 85-86, 115, 122, 125, 127, 131
Growth 70, 96, 127-128
Holy Spirit 5, 9-10, 12, 53, 56-57, 62, 69, 71, 86, 96, 100, 107
Humility 101, 109
Inerrancy 123
Inheritance 52, 56
Judas 28
Judge 51, 78, 101
Judgment 22, 24-25, 29-30, 32, 40, 47-48, 50-51, 66, 75-76, 79-80, 82-83, 86, 91, 94, 96, 102, 109-110
Justification 14, 17, 23, 25, 51-52, 63, 66-67, 79, 81, 94, 108-109, 114, 123, 131-134
Knowing God 127
Law 2, 16, 23, 61
Life 5, 9-12, 14-16, 19, 21-25, 32-33, 37, 40, 42, 45-51, 53-54, 56, 58-63, 65-67, 70-72, 77, 79-80, 82-83, 85, 87-96, 99-102, 104-112, 114, 119-120, 122, 126-127, 129, 131-134

Light ... 16, 24, 52, 57, 76, 86, 91-92, 116, 118-119, 121-123, 127-128, 132, 134
Lord 9-12, 16, 18-19, 22-25, 28-30, 35-37, 39-42, 46-53, 55-56, 63, 67, 69-71, 73-76, 78, 80, 85, 88, 90-91, 94-96, 100-101, 103-105, 107-109, 114-115, 117-121, 124-126, 128-129, 132-134
Lord's Supper 119, 126, 129
Lost 19, 65, 67, 78, 82, 89-91, 103, 117-118, 126, 128
Love ... 12, 45, 86, 117, 120-122, 127-129
MacArthur 45-46, 81, 85-86, 125
Mature 116, 121, 123, 126-127
Maturity 90, 126, 128
Ministry 35-36, 51-52, 56-57, 62, 67, 70, 72, 79-80, 90-91, 103, 134
Neighbor 123
Obedience 11, 18, 23, 25, 134
Parable 44, 67, 117
Pastors 11, 13, 31, 45, 47, 95, 129
Perseverance 82, 90
Perseverance of the Saints 82
Prayer 12, 115, 122, 125-126
Professors 105, 111
Rapture 31, 69
Reformation 15, 71, 91, 93
Regeneration 21-22, 33, 36-37, 48, 51-53, 55, 81, 94, 102, 110, 125, 131, 133
Repent 5, 9-10, 15-18, 21, 24-25, 27-33, 35-36, 39-45, 50-54, 57, 59-60, 62, 67, 73-75, 78-79, 83, 85, 88, 90-91, 93, 95-96, 99-104, 106-108, 110, 113-114, 116, 118-120, 128, 147-149, 151-154
Repentance 1-2, 5-19, 21-25, 27-33, 36-37, 40, 44-54, 56-57, 59-63, 65-67, 70-71, 73-83, 85-97, 99-119, 121, 128, 134
Rest 19, 29, 55, 125
Righteous 6, 16, 81, 101, 103, 113-115, 118-119
Righteousness 51, 75, 78, 86, 114-115, 132

Subject Index

Salvation, everlasting............................ 79
Sanctification........................ 14, 18-19, 61
Satisfaction 17
Save.................... 16, 82-83, 105, 119, 132
Saved 14, 18-19, 22, 32, 46, 49,
  55, 61, 63, 71, 74-76, 79, 82, 87-89, 99,
  102, 131-133
Saving faith...............................18, 59, 66
Savior....................................24, 50-51, 76
Secure..25, 96
Seek 11, 18, 124
Seeking..25, 79
Sign 55
Signs 45
Sin........................ 11, 16-18, 22, 25, 36,
  40, 46-47, 49, 66, 82, 86, 88, 90, 92-96,
  102, 109, 116, 120, 122, 124-125, 128,
  133
Sinners 32, 40, 101, 118, 124
Sovereign 14
Submission 27, 88
Submit 27
Substitutionary atonement................ 123

Suffering...................................67, 91, 110
Surrender... 92
Temporal.... 21-22, 25, 29, 47-48, 50, 66,
  75-76, 82-83, 86, 91, 94, 102, 109-110
Tongue 43
Transform 91
Transformation 70, 127
Transformed.. 127
Truth........ 12, 30, 76, 82-83, 86, 101, 104,
  109-110, 119, 123, 125, 128
Walking in the light............ 91, 116, 118,
  122-123, 127
Westminster Confession................ 15-16
Witness...72, 134
Works 11, 14-17, 23,
  29-30, 51-52, 66, 79, 81, 88, 90, 93-94,
  101-102, 104, 107, 115, 122-123, 131,
  133-134
Works salvation 15, 122
Worship................................ 86, 107, 122
Yoke 62

Study Guide

Chapter 1: Why Study Repentance?

1. Defend the idea that 2 Peter 3:9 is teaching that repentance is necessary to escape eternal condemnation.
2. Agree or disagree, and why: In 2 Corinthians 7:10, Paul is saying that repentance is required for everlasting life.
3. Give two or more possible interpretations of Acts 11:18.
4. Give three examples of major evangelistic tracts which say that repentance is required to be born again.
5. Give three examples of famous Evangelicals who teach that repentance is required for eternal salvation.
6. Do you think the quotations given from Grudem accurately represent the teachings of most pastors and theologians? Why or why not?
7. Was there a time in your life when you were confused about what one must do to be saved? If yes, please explain.
8. Could confusion about the doctrine of repentance keep a person from being born again? Why or why not?

Chapter 2: Repentance in Church History

1. Agree or disagree, and why: Church history does not tell us what to believe.
2. What was the Marrow Controversy about?
3. Do you agree that most in church history have taught that repentance means turning from sins? Defend your answer.

4. Agree or disagree, and why: Most in church history have taught that repentance is required to have everlasting life.
5. What is Torrance saying about the understanding of the saving message in the early church?
6. Summarize the statement on repentance in the Westminster Confession of Faith.
7. Do you agree that most Evangelicals believe that repentance is a key element in sanctification? Defend your answer.
8. Do you find Charles Stanley's statement on confession and repentance to be accurate? Why or why not?

Chapter 3: Repentance in the Old Testament

1. What is the main word for repentance in the Old Testament, and why is it important that we understand its meaning?
2. What is the clearest verse(s) in the Old Testament which indicates what one must do to be justified before God (saved from eternal condemnation)? Hint: the answer is not found in Chapter 3.
3. What does "turn and live" mean in Ezekiel 18:23, 32?
4. Put Dyer's statement in your own words.
5. Why do you think that Feinberg is so adamant in saying that Ezekiel 18 is not discussing justification/regeneration?
6. Read Jonah 3:1-10. Which verses are telling us about the repentance of the Ninevites (see Matt 12:41)?
7. What does Jonah 3:5-10 teach about repentance and salvation?
8. What two factors suggest that Isaiah 55:7 is not discussing what one must do to have everlasting life?

Chapter 4: The Meaning of Repentance in the New Testament

1. Explain how the OED went about determining the meanings of English words.
2. What does BDAG say that *metanoeō* and *metanoia* mean?
3. What do the *-strephō* words in the New Testament mean when used in relation to sins?
4. When does *turning to the Lord* refer to believing in Jesus in the New Testament? Give at least three examples.

5. Agree or disagree, and why: Judas repented after he betrayed Jesus.
6. Agree or disagree, and why: In Matthew 12:41 the Lord was saying that the Ninevites escaped temporal judgment because they turned from their evil ways.
7. Do you think that Simon the magician (Acts 8:12-24) was a messed up new believer or an unbeliever? Defend your answer.
8. Was putting on sackcloth and ashes repentance? Defend your answer.

Chapter 5: Repent for the Kingdom of Heaven Is at Hand (Matthew 3:2; 4:17)

1. How might Dispensationalism help in interpreting these two verses?
2. What did John the Baptist and the Lord Jesus mean when they said, "the kingdom of heaven is at hand"?
3. What is McNeile saying when he distinguishes between *a means of bringing the Kingdom* and *a preparation for it*?
4. If the nation had repented, they would have believed in Jesus as their Messiah Savior. Agree or disagree, and why.
5. If the nation had believed in Jesus, then they would have repented. Agree or disagree, and why.
6. Give the strongest arguments you can for the view that Matthew 3:2 and 4:17 are evangelistic verses.
7. Give the strongest arguments you can that Matthew 3:2 and 4:17 are not evangelistic verses.
8. Agree or disagree, and why: Matthew 3:2 and 4:17 do not tell us whether repentance is or is not a condition for individual regeneration.

Chapter 6: Repent and Believe in the Gospel (Mark 1:14-15)

1. What is *the gospel* in Mark 1:14-15? Defend your answer.
2. How does I. Howard Marshall understand the expression *the kingdom of God*?
3. Do you agree or disagree with Marshall's understanding of *the kingdom of God*? Defend your answer.

4. How does William MacDonald understand Mark 1:14-15?
5. Do you agree or disagree with MacDonald's understanding? Defend your answer.
6. Agree or disagree, and why: Jesus might have come again and set up His kingdom as early as AD 40.
7. Do you think it would be a good idea to use Mark 1:14-15 in an evangelistic presentation? Why or why not?
8. Some suggest that *the gospel of the kingdom* was an evangelistic message different from the Apostle Paul's gospel of justification by faith alone. They think *the gospel of the kingdom* was a form of works salvation that was in place prior to the birth of the church (when the saving message changed to faith alone). Do you agree or disagree? Defend your answer.

Chapter 7: Unless You Repent ou Will All Likewise Perish (Luke 13:3, 5)

1. What started the incident in Luke 13:1-5? What was Jesus told (Luke 13:1-2)?
2. What happened to the Galileans that Jesus was asked about?
3. What does *perish* mean in verse 3?
4. How does the word *likewise* help us understand the word *perish* in verse 3?
5. Why did Jesus bring up the incident of the eighteen who died when a tower fell on them (verse 4)? How is this connected?
6. Why does Jesus repeat verse 3 verbatim in verse 5?
7. What is it that Jesus was warning His listeners about, hell or judgment in this life? Defend your answer.
8. Agree or disagree, and why: the word *all* in Luke 13: 3, 5 refers to everyone without exception.

Chapter 8: If One Goes to Them from the Dead, They Will Repent (Luke 16:19-31)

1. How can the rich man and Lazarus both be in Hades if one is suffering torment and the other is not?
2. Do you think that this account is a parable or an actual historical incident? Defend your answer.

3. Does the torment of verse 23 refer to torment after the end of the age or torment now? Defend your answer.
4. What does Abraham say that one must do to avoid "this place of torment"?
5. What does the rich man say that one must do to avoid "this place of torment"?
6. Many commentators suggest that Abraham and the rich man are saying the same thing. Do you agree or disagree, and why?
7. Why does Abraham refer to *Moses and the prophets* (verses 29, 31)?
8. List two passages in Moses and two passages in the prophets that Abraham might have in mind. Explain why these passages apply.

Chapter 9: Repentance and Forgiveness Should Be Preached (Luke 24:47)

1. What evidence is there that this is a Great Commission verse?
2. Are all Great Commission verses calls to evangelize? Defend your answer.
3. How does John Piper understand Luke 24:47?
4. Is the preaching of forgiveness the same as the preaching of everlasting life? Defend your answer.
5. Do you think it is significant that the Lord Jesus never in John's Gospel links believing in Him and the forgiveness of sins? Why or why not?
6. What is fellowship forgiveness, and where is it found in Scripture?
7. True or false: If you are a believer in Jesus Christ, then all your sins are already forgiven. Defend your answer.
8. Is the Apostolic preaching of repentance in Acts evangelistic? Defend your answer.

Chapter 10: Repent, and You Shall Receive the Gift of the Holy Spirit (Acts 2:38)

1. Why do many think that Acts 2:38 is an evangelistic appeal?
2. What evidence is there that Acts 2:38 is not an evangelistic appeal?

3. Discuss the two issues of "cut to the heart" in Acts 2:37.
4. What is at the heart of the question in Acts 2:37, salvation or something else?
5. What evidence is there in Acts that the Holy Spirit and the forgiveness of sins sometimes did not occur at the time of the new birth?
6. Most people would think that you were crazy if you said that receiving the Holy Spirit and the forgiveness of sins did not occur at the moment of the new birth in the early chapters of Acts. Does that make you wonder if that view is right? Why or why not?
7. What is Tanton suggesting that Acts 2:38 means?
8. What do you think that Acts 2:38 means? Defend your answer.

Chapter 11: God Has Granted the Gentiles Repentance to Life (Acts 11:18)

1. When in the Acts 10 account were Cornelius and his household born again?
2. Why did the Spirit fall on these Gentiles at the very moment of faith?
3. Was it easy or hard for Peter to go these Gentiles and evangelize them? Defend your answer.
4. After this incident, Peter gets in a kerfuffle with "those of the circumcision" (Acts 11:2-3). Who are "those of the circumcision"?
5. What was their objection to what Peter did?
6. How did Peter defend his actions?
7. What are the three options about what Acts 11:18 means, and which view do you take, and why?
8. How do Peter's remarks at the Jerusalem Council (Acts 15:7-11) impact your understanding of Acts 11:18?

Chapter 12: Godly Sorrow Produces Repentance Leading to Salvation (2 Corinthians 7:10)

1. Discuss the context of 2 Corinthians 7:10.

2. Considering the context, what does the word *salvation* mean in verse 10?
3. What do you think of the statement by Hughes?
4. Why does the *New Geneva Study Bible* suggest that this verse is not an evangelistic verse?
5. What is the difference between worldly sorrow and godly sorrow?
6. Using Biblical examples, illustrate the difference between worldly sorrow and godly sorrow.
7. Considering your study of this passage, why do you think pastors and theologians would suggest that Paul is discussing the condition for everlasting life in 2 Corinthians 7:10?
8. Agree or disagree, and why: There is a knee-jerk reaction by many Evangelicals to the word *salvation*. When they see it in the Bible, their first thought is that salvation from eternal condemnation is in view.

Chapter 13: Turning to God from Idols (1 Thessalonians 1:9)

1. Do you think that the concept of repentance is found in 1 Thessalonians 1:9? Why or why not?
2. Why was Paul giving this report about the Thessalonians?
3. What does "waiting for His Son from heaven" (1 Thess 1:10) refer to? Defend your answer.
4. Agree or disagree, and why: The context here is salvific.
5. What do you think of the quotation by commentator Andy Johnson?
6. What do you think about what Hiebert said about this verse?
7. Compare 1 Thessalonians 1:9 to Ephesians 2:8-9.
8. Compare 1 Thessalonians 1:9 to Revelation 3:7-13 and to Philippians 1:3-11.

Chapter 14: God Wishes None to Perish but for All to Repent (2 Peter 3:9)

1. What does *perish* mean in 2 Peter 3:9? Defend your answer.
2. What does 2 Peter 3:9 have to say about why the Lord Jesus has delayed fulfilling "the promise of His coming"?

3. How can our understanding of 2 Peter 3:9 be enhanced by looking at the verses which precede (3:1-8) and follow (3:10-13)?
4. Why do you think so many pastors and theologians understand 2 Peter 3:9 to be discussing the condition of escaping eternal condemnation?
5. If all people prior to the Rapture are going to die physically, then how could *perish* in 2 Peter 3:9 refer to dying physically?
6. After the fall, the human life expectancy as revealed in the early chapters of Genesis was eight hundred to nine hundred years. But then after the Noahic flood, the life expectancy dropped to seventy or eighty years (Ps 90:10). How might this information impact our understanding of 2 Peter 3:9?
7. What do you think of the comment by Zane Hodges about this passage?
8. Agree or disagree, and why: 2 Peter 3:9 illustrates the truth of Ezekiel 18:23.

Chapter 15: Other Verses Thought to Link Salvation and Repentance

1. Why do most commentators think the two parables of Luke 15:1-10 are teaching that those who repent are saved from eternal condemnation?
2. What evidence is there that the two parables are teaching that believers who stray and repent are welcomed back into fellowship with God?
3. Why do many commentators think that in Acts 17:30 Paul was saying that those who repent escape eternal condemnation?
4. What evidence is there that Acts 17:30 is part of a message designed to generate interest in Jesus, but not an evangelistic message?
5. Which of the two suggested interpretations of Acts 20:21 is correct? Defend your answer.
6. Agree or disagree, and why: Paul implies in Romans 2:4 that repentance is a condition of justification before God.
7. Is Hebrews 6:4-8 directed to born-again believers or to false professors? Defend your answer.

8. What is the author of Hebrews warning about in Hebrews 6:4-8? Defend your answer.
9. Why do many commentators believe that James 5:19-20 refers to saving someone from eternal condemnation?
10. What evidence is there that James 5:19-20 refers to a believer saving a fellow believer from temporal judgment?

Chapter 16: Repentance and the Gospel of John

1. Do you think that it is significant to our understanding of the saving message that the words *repent* and *repentance* are not found in John's Gospel? Defend your answer.
2. Do you think that Grudem's suggestions regarding the concept of repentance being found in John's Gospel are valid? Why or why not?
3. Do you think that MacArthur's list regarding the concept of repentance in John has any validity? Why or why not?
4. Do you think that John 5:14 and 8:11 are calls to repentance? Why or why not?
5. If the concept of repentance is present in John's Gospel, but never in an evangelistic context, what would that suggest?
6. Do you think that an argument about silence is different from a mere argument from silence? Defend your answer.
7. Let's say that there was one passage in John which clearly states that the only condition of everlasting life is believing in Jesus (e.g., John 3:14-18). Would that one passage be enough, if it was crystal clear, to prove that nothing else is a condition of everlasting life? Why or why not?
8. List five or more passages in John's Gospel in which the Lord says that whoever believes in Him has everlasting life, shall never perish, shall never hunger, shall never thirst, or shall never die.

Chapter 17: Preaching Repentance and Salvation

1. Do you have a responsibility to teach God's Word to others? Defend your answer from Scripture.

2. In 25 words or less, state what a person must do in order to be saved from eternal condemnation.
3. If you have children, do you think it is a good idea to warn them about the dangers of straying away from the Lord? Defend your answer.
4. According to Luke 15:11-24, what are some of the negative consequences the younger son experienced when he departed into the spiritual far country? List the verse(s) in which each consequence is found.
5. Why do you think the Lord doesn't give us any details about the younger son's prodigal living?
6. How is a proper understanding of repentance an important part of having a proper Biblical mindset (Rom 12:1-2)?
7. Most pastors and theologians do not keep the message of salvation by faith separate from the message of deliverance by turning from sins. Why is it dangerous to mix these messages?
8. Agree or disagree, and why: A person who teaches that repentance is not a condition of everlasting life is inadvertently promoting a life of sin.

Chapter 18: Repentance Is a Vital Biblical Doctrine

1. Agree or disagree, and why: Church history got the doctrine of repentance wrong soon after the Apostles died.
2. In 25 words or less, state the consensus position of most Evangelicals today on the doctrine of repentance.
3. Summarize the Old Testament teaching about repentance.
4. Where are calls for national repentance found in the New Testament?
5. In what way can the teaching of repentance in our homes and churches help prevent believers from straying away from the Lord?
6. Agree or disagree, and why: The believer who is in fellowship with God does not need to repent. Therefore, a believer might remain in fellowship with God for months or even years, without ever needing to repent.
7. Agree or disagree, and why: A person who believes that in order to be born again he must believe in Jesus and turn from all his

sins is not believing the message of everlasting life that Jesus preached (e.g., John 3:16). If he has never believed that the only condition is faith in Christ, then he has not yet been born again.

8. Agree or disagree, and why: While repentance is not a condition of everlasting life, repentance can lead to a person's coming to faith in Christ and being born again.

More GES Books
www.faithalone.org

Anthony B. Badger
—*Confronting Calvinism*
—*Free Grace Theology on Trial*

Harlan Betz
—*Setting the Stage for Eternity*

Steve Elkins
—*The Roman Road Revisited: New Vistas on the Road to Resurrection Living*
—*Keys to Kingdom Greatness: An Exposition of the Sermon on the Mount*

Zane Hodges
—*Absolutely Free (2nd ed.)*
—*The Atonement and Other Writings*
—*The Epistle of James*
—*The Epistles of John*
—*Faith in His Name: Listening to the Gospel of John*
—*First Peter: The Salvation of the Soul*
—*A Free Grace Primer*
—*Grace in Eclipse*
—*The Gospel Under Siege*
—*Harmony with God*
—*Here Walks My Enemy: The Story of Luis*
—*The Hungry Inherit*
—*Jesus, God's Prophet*
—*The Journey of Faith: Sermons on Hebrews*
—*Luke (Vol 1)*
—*Luke (Vol 2)*
—*Power to Make War*
—*Power to Stand: An Exposition of Jude*
—*Romans: Deliverance from Wrath*
—*Second Peter: Shunning Error in Light of the Savior's Soon Return*
—*Six Secrets of the Christian Life (Second Edition)*
—*Spiritual Lessons from the Life of David*
—*Tough Texts: Did Jesus Teach Salvation by Works?*
—*Zane Hodges JOTGES Memorial Issue*
—*What Is the Outer Darkness?*

Lucas Kitchen
—*Eternal Rewards: It Will Pay to Obey*

Shawn Lazar
—*Beyond Doubt: How to Be Sure of Your Salvation*
—*Chosen to Serve: Why Divine Election Is to Service, Not to Eternal Life*

Bill Lee
—*Grace Recovered*

René López
—*Romans Unlocked*

C. Gordon Olson
—*Beyond Calvinism and Arminianism*

Lawrence Vance
—*The Other Side of Calvinism*

Bob Wilkin
—*Confident in Christ (2nd ed.)*
—*Four Views on the Role of Works at the Final Judgment*
—*A Gospel of Doubt: The Legacy of John MacArthur's The Gospel According to Jesus*
—*Inerrancy for Dummies*
—*Is Calvinism Biblical? Let the Scriptures Decide*
—*The Road to Reward (2nd ed.)*
—*Secure and Sure*
—*The Ten Most Misunderstood Words in the Bible*
—*Turn and Live: The Power of Repentance*

Various Authors
—*The Grace New Testament Commentary*

Kenneth W. Yates
—*Hebrews: Partners with Christ*

Made in the USA
Middletown, DE
20 July 2019